THE ANATOMY OF DOMESTIC VIOLENCE

Emily's Story

Angharad Candlin

Copyright © 2025
First Published in Australia in May 2025
By Morpheus Publishing
Geelong Victoria 3216
www.morpheuspublishing.com.au

Paperback ISBN: 978-1-7641639-7-2

Title: The Anatomy of Domestic Violence: Emily's Story
Author: Angharad Candlin
Senior Editor: Justine Martin
Editor: Lynette Reurts
Cover Graphics: Lynette Ingles
Image: Multiple Pathways To Harm used with permission

A catalogue record for this book is available from the National Library of Australia.

DISCLAIMER
The information contained in this book is for general informational purposes only. The author and publisher are not offering any medical, legal or professional advice. While every effort has been made to ensure the accuracy and completeness of the information provided, the author and publisher assume no responsibility for errors or omissions or any outcomes or consequences resulting from using this book's content.

DISTRIBUTION
This book is distributed by Morpheus Publishing and is available through authorised distributors, booksellers, Morpheus Publishing website and Angharad Candlin's website.

COPYRIGHT PERMISSIONS
For copyright permissions or any other inquiries, please contact:

PUBLISHER: Morpheus Publishing

www.morpheuspublishing.com.au | hello@morpheuspublising.com.au | +61403 564 942

AUTHOR: Angharad Candlin

https://www.angharadcandlin.com/ | hello@angharadcandlin.com

https://www.morpheuspublishing.com.au/authors/angharad-candlin

CONTENTS

FOREWORD

It feels like I have known Angharad forever. When we first met, I knew absolutely she was a part of my life that I didn't know was missing. Even though we've lived many miles apart, we have always kept in touch. When we meet, straight away it's as if we've not been apart. It's because I trust her that I've been happy to share my story, although I didn't think it was worthy, that I was worthy of the telling. I thought I'd come to terms with it.

I'm willing to tell my story so that other women and men can understand or identify with what, for years, I could not express. What stopped me in the past was shame, sadness and the experience of my own parents' relationship. I feel a huge sense of responsibility and unconditional love for my children.

I've spent my whole working life being with families and children in the classroom. I specialised in teaching children with emotional and behavioural needs and supporting their extended families. I particularly remember telling one beaten mother that no one had the right to harm her or her children. I reassured her that we and others could help them. It struck me like a ton of bricks that I should apply this to myself.

When my ex-husband had gone further along the path of domestic abuse, intimidation, control, gaslighting and almost ritualised abuse, I found myself on the other side of the table. I was used to supporting people. I found myself asking who would support me. I sat and wondered how on earth this could happen to someone like me. I had a successful career. I cared for others. It was such a terrible feeling of stupidity; he told me I was stupid. Of madness; he told me I was mad. I didn't know what to do.

I was in the situation of being in loco parentis to 40 children in my classroom, yet he eroded my rights to see my own sons and daughter every day. He spied on me, and he hid my passport, my driving licence and my educational qualification certificates. He told me I was worthless, he degraded me, and he assaulted me in every way possible. He eroded everything within me.

He had become friends with some of the boys in my social group when I met him. We were all at the pub. I noticed that he dominated the conversation around the table. He was very comfortable, confident, entertaining, slick and good-looking, and I did not like him. Fast forward a few months, I was back from university, and I started to see him in a different light. He homed in on me, smothered me with attention and love, and yet almost immediately became jealous with respect to my male friends.

We had to leave early from events because, as he put it, I had behaved badly. It was the start of an extremely slippery slope, and I started to lose myself. He always said sorry. He said it was because he loved me so much. Angharad immediately had misgivings about him, so much so that she had a quiet word with him on our wedding day. I wasn't aware of this but I did notice he had taken a sudden dislike to my best friend.

Another pattern I see clearly now is how he alienated me from my friends. I feel dramatic saying he abused me in many insidious ways. I began to feel I was defective and incompetent. I justified his behaviour because I felt that I was impaired. There are so many examples and Angharad has detailed some of them in this book.

I found the process of writing this book with Angharad distressing as I dug back down into the fog of murkiness and desolation. And to open doors I thought I'd firmly shut and never wanted to open again. I did my best to protect my children and my grandmother, even when I was not home with them. Still, I'm plagued by thoughts that maybe I could have continued to live under these circumstances. Maybe I should have persevered.

Many of my friends thought I was lucky in my life. I had a lovely house, a good job, and many opportunities, and my children all succeeded. They said I should have been grateful. I cannot thank Angharad enough for allowing me to feel angry. For believing me.

Thank you for reassuring me that this wasn't my fault and for giving me an opportunity to tell my story. My truth.

What finally made him leave was that I became ill and disfigured and "ugly", having had surgery for a brain injury and cancer. He just didn't want to have, as he put it, a "cripple" on his hands. I believe that he thought he was lucky. Who would disbelieve or criticise a man who was going through all of this with a brain-injured, cancer-ridden wife?

I really want women who read this book to know that they're not stupid or dumb. To not believe the lies that have been spoken to them and about them. They don't deserve any of it. I want them to know that there are places that they can go for help and support. Abusers seek out wounded birds. They seek out someone who is vulnerable. They have a nose for it. It is not your fault.

Writing this book with Angharad has been hard, so hard; however, it gave me an opportunity to confront my experiences. I have some excellent professionals around me who are helping me to heal. I desperately want to do something worthwhile for the rest of my life. I won't be able to teach again, but I hope that I can become an advocate and support others who have been through the same thing I have.

I had a fortunate start to my life. I really was very lucky. And now I have a fortunate life again. I don't have to look over my shoulder anymore. I have a little place of my own with good friends around me. I am a smiley person. I was always a smiley person, but if I was too chatty, too smiley, he would give me that look. That look told me I was doing something he didn't approve of. But now I can be smiley again. I can be joyous. I am thankful.

Love,
Emily

Angharad Candlin

INTRODUCTION

My friend Emily and I were in our early twenties when she got married. It was a small wedding with family and a few close friends. After the speeches, I saw her new husband standing alone near the cake table. I went over to him and quietly said, *"If you ever hurt her, you will have me to answer to"*.

I don't make a habit of threatening my friends' husbands, but there was something about him that made all of my alarm bells ring.

If I had known then what I know now, I would have done everything in my power to stop the marriage. As a 22-year-old psychology student, I didn't know about domestic violence. I didn't know about coercive control. I didn't know about gaslighting. I didn't know about the precise and purposeful annihilation inflicted by a perpetrator upon a victim-survivor. I didn't know the anatomy of domestic violence. I do now.

This book is about one of my best friends, Emily. It is her story of domestic violence. I have wanted to write this book for some years, but it was a random video call that I had with Emily about nine months ago that set the wheels in motion. Emily FaceTimed me late one night. I was actually just leaving the Emergency Department at my local hospital. I'd been bitten by something and had a big reaction to it. Emily was concerned for me but also laughed heartily about my ridiculous situation. She seemed to be in a good place, so I floated the idea of this book to her. She agreed. She hadn't been ready before, but she was now.

The significant issues that will become apparent throughout the telling of Emily's story are not only the utter failure of every comprehensive system that is in place to protect victims of crime but also the "systems abuse" that Emily and her children experienced. There were dozens of opportunities for professionals in protective systems to intervene, but in reality, they actively worked against Emily and her children and placed them in even more danger. As her friend and as someone who worked in the community for decades, I am utterly furious and desperate about the prevalence of domestic violence and what she has gone through.

When you simultaneously view all of the individual elements that should have worked to support this whole family, including the perpetrator, the systemic neglect of vulnerable members of the community comes into sharp focus. Having carefully pieced together this decades-long jigsaw puzzle, my biggest surprise, quite frankly, is that Emily is still alive.

We are taking a risk by sharing Emily's story. We have made every effort to disguise people and places. Every name, except my own, has been changed. Locations have been changed; I have chosen places that reflect similar attributes. Some of the time periods have been altered slightly. However, the facts remain accurate.

The risk is that the perpetrator will once again weaponise the court system, as he so often has done, in his ongoing efforts to control Emily and stop this story from being told. Victim-survivors of domestic violence have their voices taken away. I have a voice. I will use it. Emily is finding her voice again, and she will use hers.

Why talk about domestic violence?

In 2024:

- 78 women were murdered in Australia.*
- 101 Australian women were murdered across the world.**
- 80% of women who died knew the perpetrator.
- 80% of women who died were mothers.
- 46 adults were victims of intimate partner homicide; 37 were women, 9 were men[1].

---

1   https://www.aic.gov.au/statistics/homicide-in-australia

In Australia, we are fortunate to have two platforms that are meticulous in their count of women who have been murdered.

*Destroy the Joint's Counting Dead Women[2] is a volunteer-run project who are very careful in the way they count the number of women in Australia who have been murdered. They will only count the death if criminal charges have been laid or there is strong evidence that the woman died as a result of violence. They count all violent deaths of women, whether it is as a result of domestic violence or not and irrespective of whether the perpetrator was male or female. They have been counting the deaths of women since 2012 and say that over 80% of violent deaths of women are a result of domestic violence.

**Australian Femicide Watch/The Red Heart Campaign[3], like Destroy the Joint, is a volunteer group run by journalist Sherele Moody. She accurately tracks the violent deaths of all Australian women and children regardless of the country of death.

Whether the deaths occurred in Australia or the rest of the world, all of the perpetrators were male. In one case, a woman was involved in the planning of the murder that her male partner committed.

In 2024, The Guardian UK[4] newspaper followed Australia's lead in conducting its own count of murdered women. Given this opportunity, it is worthwhile briefly comparing the two jurisdictions. Accounting for population size, in 2023/2024, Australia and the UK had almost equal numbers of male murder victims. Notably, in 2024, when adjusted for population size, Australia recorded nearly twice the proportion of female murder victims compared to the UK — 23% versus 13%.

Domestic violence is insidious. Nothing any government has done anywhere in the world has been able to stop it. Domestic violence can only be stopped when all of us together, men and women alike, gather our collective voices in a rising crescendo of "Enough is enough!".

---

2 https://www.facebook.com/DestroyTheJoint

3 https://www.facebook.com/TheREDHEARTCampaign

4 https://www.theguardian.com/uk-news/ng-interactive/2024/dec/31/killed-women-count-a-project-highlighting-the-toll-and-tragedy-of-violence-against-women-in-the-uk

A significant issue is the community's lack of understanding of domestic violence in and of itself. We still hear the refrain, *"Why doesn't she leave?"* We never hear the words, *"Why does he abuse women and children?"* We still hear the chorus of *"He must have snapped."* We never hear, *"He chose to use violence."* We still hear the deafening cacophony of *"She didn't protect her children".* We never hear, *"He used violence as a parenting choice".*

These examples are gendered because the statistics show us clearly that men regularly murder women. Men also murder men. Women hardly ever murder men or women. Yes, there are always exceptions to any rule, but when we allow the exceptions to lessen the impact of the status quo, we are guaranteeing that women and children will continue to be the victim of male violence. It behoves everyone to be educated in this area, and an exceptionally helpful, although incredibly difficult to read, resource is the Domestic Violence Death Review Reports[5]. The team who work on these reports go into highly focussed detail to assist the community to fully understand the nature of Domestic Violence.

Having said that, it is more helpful to use the non-gendered language of perpetrator or abuser and victim-survivor so that we don't get distracted by side issues. This book is about a male perpetrator and a female victim-survivor, but there are definitely situations where the opposite is true.

The term "domestic violence" can be a troublesome one. Often, people don't realise that there are many aspects to domestic violence over and above physical assault. The term domestic abuse is becoming more common and is arguably more nuanced, covering the full spectrum of violent behaviour. Other terms that are used are domestic and family violence, family violence or intimate partner violence. Given that domestic violence is commonly used within the community, I will continue to use it throughout this book, except when I am quoting particular sources.

---

5   https://coroners.nsw.gov.au/documents/reports/DVDRT_Annual_
     Report_2021-23.pdf

According to the NSW Crimes (Domestic and Personal Violence) Act 2007[6], "*Domestic Abuse encompasses the following behaviour towards someone with whom they have a "domestic relationship":*

- *Violent or threatening behaviour.*
- *Behaviour that coerces or controls the second person.*
- *Behaviour that causes the second person to fear for the other person's safety or wellbeing or the safety and wellbeing of others.*

As well as engaging in or threatening to engage in:

- *Behaviour that is physically abusive or violent.*
- *Behaviour that is sexually abusive, coercive or violent.*
- *Behaviour that is economically or financially abusive.*
- *Behaviour that is verbally abusive.*
- *Behaviour that shames, degrades, or humiliates.*
- *Behaviour that is intimidation.*
- *Behaviour that is stalking or harasses or monitors or tracks a person's activities, whether physical or using technology or any other way.*
- *Behaviour that damages or destroys property.*
- *Behaviour that causes death or injury to an animal or otherwise makes use of an animal to threaten a person.*
- *Behaviour that prevents the second person from doing the following or isolates them from:*

    o *Making or keeping connections with the person's family, friends or culture.*
    o *Participating in cultural or spiritual ceremonies or practices.*
    o *Expressing the person's cultural identity.*

---

6   https://legislation.nsw.gov.au/view/whole/html/inforce/current/act-2007-080

- *Behaviour that deprives the second person of liberty or unreasonably controls or regulates a person's day-to-day activities,*

- *Behaviour that causes a child to hear or witness or otherwise be exposed to the effects of the above behaviour.*

Furthermore, "Domestic Abuse" can be a single act, omission or circumstance or a combination of acts, omissions or circumstances over a period of time. All of these behaviours may constitute domestic abuse even if the behaviour does not constitute a criminal offence."

Jurisdictions across the Western world have very similar pieces of legislation.

Using the Safe and Together model to address domestic violence

Safe and Together is a framework developed by David Mandel and the Safe and Together Institute[7] to address the nuances of domestic violence that are so often missed. It is arguably the most respected and comprehensive model available today to address the impacts of domestic violence. There are numerous short online courses that the Safe and Together Institute have made available as well as the longer and much more comprehensive training that practitioners in the field undertake.

In this book, whilst I am sharing Emily's story, I am using the framework of Safe and Together as a means of understanding the true nature of domestic violence. If we can identify the pattern of abusive behaviours that perpetrators display, then we can all become more aware of the anatomy of domestic violence and maybe, just maybe, we can create a world where everyone is safer.

The foundational principle of Safe and Together is to work with the non-offending parent to keep them safe and together with their children. We can only do that if we understand, with absolute clarity, how perpetrators of domestic violence control the protective parent.

I have been trained in Safe and Together. I have been trained in the supervision of practitioners who use Safe and Together. Along

---

7   https://safeandtogetherinstitute.com

with a valued colleague, I have facilitated professional development and supervision for over 100 trained practitioners to embed Safe and Together in their work. I have never been employed by Safe and Together, nor do I work for them in any capacity.

Whilst not all domestic violence occurs within the realms of a family with children, the Safe and Together framework encompasses children because the majority of domestic violence occurs within a family environment, and children, generally speaking, are the invisible victim-survivors of domestic violence. The majority of the Safe and Together principles can be used in situations where a couple has no children or when the individuals involved are not in a "couple" relationship per se but are sharing a house. Where children are not involved, the use of the term "child" can, for the most part, be interchanged with the term "victim-survivor".

The key principles of Safe and Together are:

1. *Keeping the child safe and together with the non-offending parent.*

2. *Partnering with the non-offending parent as a default position.*

3. *Intervening with the perpetrator to reduce risk and harm to the child.*

The critical components of Safe and Together are to understand the following:

- *Perpetrator's pattern of coercive control.*

- *Actions taken by the perpetrator to harm the child.*

- *Full spectrum of non-offending parent's efforts to promote child safety and wellbeing.*

- *The adverse impact of the perpetrator's behaviour on the child.*

- *Role of substance abuse, mental health, culture and other social-economic factors.*

There are many articles and an increasing amount of research that have been produced about domestic violence. In the scheme of things, not many books have been written, certainly not enough, that peel back the layers, over decades, of one person's story and the lifelong devastation that domestic violence brings.

What does the data tell us?

Whilst data can be quite dry, and I certainly don't intend to labour the point in this book, it is important to have a clear understanding of the numbers around violence. I invite you to stay with me for a few minutes as I unpack just how prevalent domestic violence is. I have tried to be as accurate as I can in detailing the statistics relating to domestic violence and take responsibility if any inaccuracies come to light.

Although my aim is to not use gendered language, I will shift for a moment into the gendered language of male perpetrators of violence.

The data clearly indicates that almost all generic violence is perpetrated by men. The largest number of victims of male violence are males, followed by females. Violence is a gendered issue. All violence, irrespective of gender, is unacceptable. The most common phrase we use when we talk about violence is "violence against women". We need to consider changing our language to "men's violence", which more accurately describes the situation.

According to the latest Australian Bureau of Statistics figures[8]:

- *79% of male victims of violence were assaulted by a male*
- *60% of female victims of violence were assaulted by a male*

When considering domestic violence, the August 2024 Prime Minister and Cabinet report[9] Unlocking the Prevention Potential: accelerating action to end domestic, family and sexual violence is useful in understanding the social structures around domestic violence.

---

8   https://www.abs.gov.au/statistics/people/crime-and-justice/crime-victimisation/latest-release

9   https://www.pmc.gov.au/sites/default/files/resource/download/unlocking-the-prevention-potential-4.pdf. Page 27

"Men who strongly endorse norms that reflect socially dominant forms of masculinity were more than:

- *8 times more likely to have perpetrated sexual violence*
- *5 times more likely to have perpetrated physical violence against an intimate partner."*

Further:

- *"1 in 4 women and 1 in 14 men have experienced violence and emotional abuse by an intimate partner since the age of 15.*
- *1 in 5 women and 1 in 16 men have experienced sexual violence since the age of 15.*
- *Almost 4 out of 5 domestic violence offenders were male.*
- *Where children were murdered as a result of domestic violence, 68% of offenders were male.*
- *80% of women report that their former partner had replaced physical abuse with financial abuse post-separation.*
- *32% of hospitalisations due to assault were related to domestic violence".*

In September 2015, then-Prime Minister Malcolm Turnbull said, *"Let me say this to you: disrespecting women does not always result in violence against women. But all violence against women begins with disrespecting women."*[10]

There are always issues with statistics. Generally speaking, perpetrators of domestic violence rarely voluntarily admit that they use violence. Victim-survivors of domestic violence (male and female), in many cases, do not come forward and self-identify as victim-survivors. Given that, the real figures of domestic violence can never fully be known. The reported numbers are generally gleaned from formal reporting mechanisms such as statistics relating to the

---

10 https://www.smh.com.au/politics/federal/malcolm-turnbulls-scathing-attack-on-men-who-commit-domestic-violence-20150924-gjtpqt.html

involvement of police, courts, non-government agencies, health and other government departments.

There is a loud minority of mostly men, who tend to use language such as:

- What about men?
- Men are victim-survivors too.
- Men may not be murdered, but they take their own lives as a result of domestic violence.

I am not saying that this isn't true; I will never say this isn't true. However, we have a few problems with the data. We cannot count these statistics if men don't come forward. Until men come forward, we can only work on guesstimates.

Yes, some men are victim-survivors of domestic violence, and we should never minimise the impact on them; all violence is unacceptable and devastating. It is, however, women who, overwhelmingly, are murdered by the men they know. It is this fact that brings us to the point where we can confidently describe domestic violence and domestic homicide as a gendered issue.

Emily and I hope that this book will assist our readers in deeply understanding domestic violence so that their voices can join with practitioners to effectively support victim-survivors to be safe (and together with their children).

ONE

This book is essentially a case study of domestic violence, which occurred over an almost 40-year period of time. It is an unflinching examination of how domestic violence strips the victim-survivor down to a shadow. Statistics and data around domestic violence are bountiful, and I have used them throughout this book to demonstrate how pervasive domestic violence is to give insight into some of Emily's experiences. But real stories can tell us so much more than data. Data is essential, but statistics don't tell us what, how, why, where, or even when. It is only by looking at the lived experience that we can unpack what the data tells us. To give us a complete picture of the depth and breadth of domestic violence and coercive control.

At its core, though, this book is my best friend's memoir. Within, there are some horrific examples of the abuse that Emily endured over her 26 year marriage and beyond. I warn the reader in advance, but I also invite the reader to sit with the ugliness so that they can comprehend the reality for every single victim-survivor of domestic violence.

I struggled with how much detail to provide and sought the advice of colleagues who work in the sector and friends who have experienced it. The consensus was to be fully open and honest. My friends who have lived with domestic violence all had a common view: too often, domestic violence is sanitised or simply alluded to. Rarely are the details explored. Firstly, it is important not to "upset" the victim-survivors, and secondly, it is important not to "upset" the general community.

As a retired psychologist who has worked alongside domestic violence and child protection for decades, my response is we can't "upset" victim-survivors. They're already "upset". They know exactly what has happened to themselves and generally have absolute solidarity with other victim-survivors. After all, they are the only ones who truly understand what it is like. They want the community to know. They want to be seen. It is only when people know the truth that they can do something.

The second reason is that domestic violence is pervasive. No one should ignore it. No one should turn their back on it. It should upset us. If we are to have any chance of changing the story, we have to look at the situation squarely in the face and feel uncomfortable. Very uncomfortable. It is only our discomfort that will prompt us all to make a difference. It is also important that we look it in the face because victim-survivors look it in the face every day. They don't have the luxury of looking away or switching off the news. The very least we can do is not turn away.

Given the data on domestic violence, it is highly likely that we all have a connection to domestic violence, whether we know it or not. A colleague, a friend, a family member, ourselves. Any and all of them could be victim-survivors or perpetrators. Domestic violence is literally everywhere.

Having worked in the community sector for over 30 years, I can speak to those overt cases of domestic violence we can all see if we open our eyes where you can see the bruises, the bashed and broken bodies—families living in poverty, drug and alcohol addictions and generational trauma. Child protection reports and children removed into statutory care. These are the cliched scenarios people think of when they hear the words domestic violence.

The risk is the stereotypes tell us only a small part of the story. If we can explain away domestic violence as a reaction to poverty or to inadequate housing or to unemployment or mental illness, it becomes something that happens to "others". When we can explain it away by socio-economic factors, we miss the truth. The truth is that perpetrating domestic violence is a choice.

Almost invisible is the domestic violence that sits beneath the surface. Hidden by a cloak of respectability, middle-class families, educated families. Families living in lovely houses in nice suburbs. People with well-paying jobs, mums and dads dropping the kids at school, attending the school musicals, helping with the school canteen, and dropping kids off at football or dance practice. Watching kids at weekend sports, going to Church or the Synagogue or the Mosque. Coffee with friends, drinks at the pub, BBQs in the backyard with extended family. Apparently loving couples who smile and hold hands, who go to functions together, who live in nice apartments with professional careers. The picture-perfect affluent family or couple are just as likely to carry the secret of violence and coercive control behind the front door as others are of love and support.

The extreme risk of coercive control behind front doors is that there are few obvious signs of the abuse being perpetrated. There are rarely visible bruises. The perpetrator is seen publicly as likeable, affable, even warm and generous. Nobody "has eyes" on this family, and the first time anyone is aware of the violence that has been perpetrated is when the victim is murdered.

The general community is shocked and horrified that this has happened because everyone had their eyes closed. No one took the signs seriously. Perhaps the victim-survivor contacted the police, but they were dismissed. Perhaps the school was concerned about the behaviour of the perpetrator but didn't raise the matter with authorities, either police or the child protection system. Perhaps they did, but the matter wasn't considered serious enough to warrant investigation. Perhaps a neighbour was concerned about the partner's behaviour but felt awkward raising it. Perhaps they did raise it, but the victim-survivor said everything was ok.

This book has been incredibly difficult for both Emily and myself to write. We have been committed to accuracy, so it has taken time to craft. Fortunately, Emily kept notes at key moments in her life, which she still has, along with a timeline of events and some life story work that she created during her stays in various residential programs. I have been very aware of the need to care for Emily and ensure she is supported psychologically whilst I have written her story. She and I have read the chapters together, and she has attended regular therapy sessions. Whilst it has been immensely painful for her, it has also been cathartic.

During our interviews and increasing video calls, it has been reassuring to see Emily's mental health slowly improve as she finally has an opportunity to make sense of her life with someone she trusts. Whilst I can never be her psychologist or counsellor, my skills and training mean I can sit with her in the mess and help her process the memories and experiences. She is committed to telling her story so that the general community can be educated and she can give a voice to the millions of victim-survivors of domestic violence whose voices have been silenced.

We are all in Emily's debt for her bravery in telling her story. It is raw, and it is agonising. It is an invitation for everyone who reads it to do something, anything, to aim for a world free of domestic violence. Every little step, every small conversation works towards ending domestic violence.

I migrated to Sydney from the United Kingdom on Christmas Eve 1990. My parents, younger brother and sister had moved here 3 years prior in the southern hemisphere winter of 1987. My older sister and I were in the middle of our university degrees in the UK, so we stayed behind to complete them. Our family left the UK at the start of the UK summer, and then a month later, once the academic year had finished, my sister and I followed for a holiday.

We arrived in Sydney at the start of winter, which was quite a shock to the system. As I explained in my book Bugger Bugger Shit: my quest for resilience, my sister had been diagnosed with a malignant melanoma in 1983. She had been in remission until just prior to our family's migration.

Dad had been employed as an academic at one of Sydney's universities, and the staff in his department were eager to welcome the entire family to Australia and help us feel at home. Some were aware of my sister's cancer diagnosis and relapse and were exceptionally kind and supportive. Various colleagues of my dad had organised some social events to help us settle in and get to know people. It was at one of these events that I met Emily.

Emily was approaching the end of her final year at school, and I had just finished my first year at university. Not knowing anyone else, and given that Emily and I were very close in age, I was relieved to see a friendly face. She was also relieved to see someone her own age, having been "gently persuaded" by her parents to come. We gravitated towards each other and hit it off immediately. We quickly made the decision to grab some food and drinks and separate ourselves from the younger children and adults.

I remember the two of us finding lots in common, particularly around music. Emily had a passion for UK bands so we enthusiastically talked about our shared appreciation for the Psychedelic Furs, David Bowie and Talking Heads. She introduced me to Crowded House, for which I will be forever grateful. We arranged to catch up again and saw quite a lot of each other over the 2 months I was in Sydney. Our friendship was cemented, and when I returned to London, we started to write quite regularly to each other - no internet or emails in the late 1980s, so we had to rely on Australia Post and the Royal Mail.

I talked to Emily about the cancer that was ravaging my sister's body and would eventually kill her in November 1987. Emily told me about the brain cancer her mum had developed and, by terrible coincidence, had also returned. Through her letters, Emily became my rock. I think this shared experience of loved ones with cancer was one of the things that connected us so deeply. Hardly anyone in our individual circles of friends could understand what we were going through, so we were both relieved to share our experiences and emotions with someone who truly "got it".

I returned to Sydney for Christmas, about a month after my sister died. Emily and I quickly caught up with each other at her house. By now, her mum was in palliative care but wanted to die at home. Emily's dad had organised for a hospital bed at home and community nurses were coming in a couple of times a day. Emily's maternal grandmother moved into the family home, and between them, she and Emily nursed Mary, Emily's mum. Emily's dad continued to work daily, and Emily's younger sister, now aged 15, struggled to comprehend what was happening. To be honest, everyone struggled to comprehend what was happening. Mary died a few weeks after Christmas. She was in her forties, far too young to die, leaving two teenage daughters and her mother totally bereft.

I still remember Mary's funeral over 30 years later. The wake was held at the family home, which was filled with dozens of people. Most of whom Emily didn't even know, and I certainly didn't. Quite a few of Emily's friends attended despite being ordered not to by their school principal. It was hard for them to know what to say. I think because, as teenagers or young adults, they had no idea how to be around their friend. I, of course, did, having been through it so recently with my sister. As we had done when we first met six months previously, Emily and I grabbed a plate of food and some drinks and disappeared to her bedroom to be by ourselves. Emily was absolutely devastated, and I had no words to help her. I hope that my presence helped.

Emily's father, on the other hand, had been having an affair. One of many, it turned out. Unbeknownst to me, he had previously left the family to live with the woman he was currently seeing but had moved back in when Mary's cancer had returned. A few days after the funeral, Emily and I had been out with her friends at a pub. We returned to her house late to find her father cuddling on the sofa with his lover. He had no concerns about the optics of this nor how it might have impacted his daughters or his mother-in-law.

I was absolutely furious with his behaviour. Emily was devastated. As young women, however, we had no way of articulating the enormity of our emotions. Mary's mother had agreed to stay in the house to care for her granddaughters, but this was too much for her, so she moved back to her own home, betrayed and outraged by the behaviour of her son-in-law. Emily and Susannah, her younger sister, were left to cope alone.

TWO

In December, prior to Mary's death, Emily's HSC results came in. Despite the stress on her during the exam period, her results were high enough for her to be accepted into an English literature degree at the Australian National University in Canberra. She was absolutely delighted about this new phase in her life. Her excitement at starting university provided some respite from her overwhelming grief. In early February, Emily packed up her belongings and moved into a shared house in Canberra. I returned to London at the end of January, ready for the second term of my second year.

Emily previously had one serious boyfriend when she was in Years 11 and 12 at school. I met him briefly during my first trip to Sydney. He seemed nice enough. Emily certainly liked him a lot, although he was quite distant and not particularly affectionate or demonstrative. Their relationship ended reasonably amicably after they both finished their HSC.

Emily and I continued with our letter writing, filling each other in on our university escapades. Emily started university and absolutely loved it. She made new friends, particularly with one of her flatmates, a girl called Jen. She also maintained relationships with the friends she had made through school. Most of them stayed in Sydney to attend university, so they continued to socialise together, with Emily joining them on weekends at home and during the university breaks.

In her letters, she also started to talk about a man she had met through one of her school friends. He was a couple of years older than her, originally from Tasmania and studying at the University of New South Wales. I didn't know then, but he was the man who was to become her abuser.

I returned to Sydney in December 1988. During my holiday, I was really happy to catch up with Emily, my one Australian friend who was back home in Sydney for the long summer holidays. What quickly became apparent to me was that Emily's father was increasingly absent, both emotionally and physically. He worked full-time and continued his relationship with the woman I had met the year previously, just after Mary's funeral.

His expectation of Emily was clearly that she take the place of his wife as the homemaker, despite now living in Canberra. She returned home almost every weekend and cared for her younger sister, did the washing and cleaned the house. The only thing she didn't actually do was the large weekly shop. I was convinced this was purely because she couldn't drive, rather than her father taking any parental responsibility.

Her dad was oblivious to the needs of his daughters; either his youngest daughter, who was struggling to manage her grief and her school work or his oldest daughter, who was trying to forge her own adult identity and study for her degree.

Emily and I became close despite the fact that I was living in the UK. She is still one of my best friends, nearly 40 years later. Our shared grief, me for my sister and she for her mother, and love of the same bands may have been the cementing of our friendship, but over time, it became so much deeper. We enjoyed the same books, movies, food, sense of humour and passion for social justice.

At some point, during a discussion about Anne of Green Gables, we described ourselves as kindred spirits. Emily said I was like Anne Shirley with my long red hair. Her long dark hair obviously meant that she was Diana. I, however, didn't have any particularly ambitious dreams or plans. Having spent my childhood moving between countries, I was quite satisfied with staying in one place, finding a job that I liked, getting married and having children, just like Diana.

On the other hand, Emily planned to travel the world, like Anne Shirley. She wanted to go to the UK and walk in the footsteps of the Brontë sisters. She dreamt of visiting Chile, where Isabel Allende was born.

Our personalities are very similar to the characters in the Anne of Green Gables books. I have a fiery temper and am outspoken and stubborn. Emily, on the other hand, has to be one of the kindest and sweetest people I know. At the time, I hardly ever heard her speak a critical word about anyone. She was even able to forgive her father for his crass behaviour following her mother's funeral.

As it turns out, I am the one who had international adventures just like my red-headed counterpart, and Emily stayed at home, got married and had babies, just like her kind, dark-haired counterpart. Oh, how I wish things had been different.

Emily and I caught up with each other the day after I arrived in Sydney for the Christmas holidays. Both of our families attended a work Christmas party. We found each other, grabbed some mince pies, christmas cake and a glass of champagne each and looked for somewhere to sit down. All of the seats were taken. I was suffering from a severe case of jet lag and was really too tired to stand up. Emily spotted a table at the side of the room, so we made a beeline for it and sat on the floor underneath it with our mince pies and champagne. This incident is one of our core shared memories; we didn't even discuss whether to sit on top of the table or under it. We both simultaneously sat on the floor, reversed backwards, leaning against the wall and didn't move for several hours.

Of course, as a young twenty-something-year-old woman, I wanted to hear all about the new man Emily had mentioned in her letters. She had met him at a pub with a group of people when she was back home in Sydney for the Easter break. Her first impression of him was that he was conceited, arrogant and full of his own self-importance. She was not at all impressed or attracted to him, and because they were in a group, it was easy for her to avoid him.

In the July holidays, he and Emily crossed paths once again. Both of them attended a party that one of her school friends held. It was a small but reasonably drunken event. At one point, the group decided they would play a childhood party game; "murder in the dark". Emily found herself hiding behind a thick curtain, and this man snuck in and kissed her out of the blue. Emily thought that it was a bold move, but she quite liked it, and her initial negative feelings began to dissipate.

Despite attending the University of New South Wales in Sydney's Eastern suburbs, he lived in the same northern Sydney suburb as Emily and her friends. Unlike his student peers, he didn't go back home for the holidays and stayed in Sydney. By the September university break of that year, he had become increasingly involved with her circle of friends.

Emily's initial dislike of him waned as she observed him in social situations. He was confident, charming and funny. He continued to flirt with her, and she began to reciprocate. Before too long, he had asked her out on a date, and their relationship quickly evolved. Her new boyfriend very quickly and repeatedly told her how much he loved and adored her. He said she was perfect, they were made for each other, and they would be together forever.

This showering of attention, romantic gestures and compliments is commonly known as "love bombing". The two significant men in her life so far - her father and first boyfriend - were distant and undemonstrative. Emily was, unsurprisingly, swept away by this good-looking and charming man.

He also said, in the midst of this love bombing, "*If we ever part, I will destroy you. I will obliterate you from my memory.*" When we were writing this book, Emily recounted the phrase so matter of factly it was chilling. I asked her to repeat it, sure that I had misheard her. She told me again, word for word. I asked again, "*He said he would destroy you?*" She said he had used that exact phrase so often throughout their marriage it was imprinted on her brain. Of course, within the context of the first time he said the sentence, it was presented as an affectionate, somewhat passionate declaration of love. It was only later that his true intention became clear. I was horrified that someone would say that to another person, least of all to my lovely, kind friend Emily.

Emily recalls that once she had returned to university in Canberra, he came to visit almost immediately. They went out for coffee and then to a little craft market. They were looking at a stall selling jewellery, and he asked her which one of two necklaces she liked. She chose one. He secretly purchased both for her and presented her with them. Emily thought it was very sweet, but in actual fact, it was the start of his careful and calculated grooming of her.

Emily and her boyfriend had been dating for about five months the first time he assaulted her. She was back in Sydney for the long summer holidays, and they went to a party one of her school friends was hosting. Her former boyfriend was there, and they chatted briefly. Emily's new boyfriend saw this, and she could tell by the look on his face that he wasn't impressed and was clearly jealous. She made a mental note to avoid spending time with her ex-boyfriend - after all, she didn't want to upset her current boyfriend.

As they left the party, her boyfriend twisted her arm behind her back and marched her back to her home. He railed at her that she was being flirtatious with the men, Emily's childhood and adolescent friends. She was *"showing him up"*. She was his girlfriend, and she needed to remember that.

Emily was utterly taken aback and shocked by this completely uncharacteristic outburst. For the first time in her life, she was afraid of someone, and this someone was her boyfriend. She had no idea what to do, and she had no script for this situation. He left her at home, terrified and confused. The next morning, whilst he didn't apologise, he did say his behaviour was *"a bit over the top"*. He then went back to being the loving and caring man she had come to know.

This was just the first of a catalogue of events where he did something similar. He never apologised. He just went back to love-bombing her. Over time, Emily would recognise when she had stepped out of line. She talked about him having a look.

When I was a practitioner, when I worked alongside domestic violence, one of the most chilling comments a victim-survivor could say to me was, *"He looked at me."*

There is a long-standing yardstick used in Commonwealth Law: the man on the Clapham omnibus. A fictitious character with which to judge behaviour in a court of law. Would the reasonable man on the Clapham omnibus consider this situation to be unacceptable? Unfortunately, this idea of what a reasonable person would think of this behaviour has been used for decades to minimise coercive control. If you were to say to the "reasonable person" on the bus, *"he looked at me"*, the likelihood is that it would be dismissed. So what if he looked at you? Young children say all the time, *"he/she looked at me"* as an explanation of why they are distressed. The adults then metaphorically roll their eyes and tell the child to ignore it.

This is what has been going on for decades when external systems, particularly the legal systems, have considered domestic violence. It is, quite frankly, a significant reason why we are in the dire situation we are currently in across the world when it comes to domestic violence. People who do not understand domestic violence simply do not understand the anatomy of coercive control. They do not understand that the phrase *"he looked at me"* is terrifying because within that look is the clear understanding that violence will follow, unbeknownst to anyone else.

The NSW Domestic Violence Legislation[11] states:

"domestic abuse means any of the following behaviours directed by one person (the first person) against another person (the second person) with whom the first person has a domestic relationship—

- *Violent or threatening behaviour.*

- *Behaviour that coerces or controls the second person.*

- *Behaviour that causes the second person to fear for the person's safety or wellbeing, or the safety and wellbeing of others.*

The types of relationships the legislation refers to are people who are:[12]

- *In an intimate personal relationship (including being married or in a de facto relationship), whether or not the relationship was of a sexual nature.*

- *In an intimate relationship, marriage or de facto relationship with the same person (for example, a person's ex-partner and current partner would have a domestic relationship with each other at law, even if they had never met).*

- *Living in the same household.*

---

11 https://legislation.nsw.gov.au/view/whole/html/inforce/current/act-2007-080 6A 1

12 https://legislation.nsw.gov.au/view/whole/html/inforce/current/act-2007-080 5

- *Living in long-term residential facilities such as aged care homes.*

- *Dependent in paid or unpaid caring relationships.*

- *Relatives (i.e. are family).*

- *For Aboriginal and Torres Strait Islander people, extended family or kin according to the Indigenous kinship system of the person's culture.*

Fortunately, the legal system is finally catching up. In recent years, there has been an increasing acceptance of how dangerous coercive control is. In a number of jurisdictions, we are seeing the passing of laws specifically focused on coercive control. The significance of the coercive control amendments is that they look at the perpetrator's pattern of behaviour or "*course of conduct*" rather than single incidents, even if the specific "*behaviour does not constitute a criminal offence*". It is also clear that threats of abuse are included.

It is worth specifying the types of behaviour that constitute abuse because many people are not aware of the breadth of the legislation and, like Emily, may not be aware that their previous or current experiences are defined as abuse.[13]

- *Behaviour that is physically abusive or violent.*

- *Behaviour that is sexually abusive, coercive or violent.*

- *Behaviour that is economically or financially abusive.*

- *Withholding financial support necessary for meeting the reasonable living expenses of a person or another person living with or dependent on the person in circumstances in which the person is dependent on financial support to meet the person's living expenses.*

- *Preventing, or unreasonably restricting or regulating, a person seeking or keeping employment or having access to or*

---

13 https://legislation.nsw.gov.au/view/whole/html/inforce/current/act-2007-080 6A2

control of the person's income or financial assets, including financial assets held jointly with another person.

- *Behaviour that is verbally abusive.*
- *Behaviour that shames, degrades or humiliates.*
- *Behaviour that is intimidation.*
- *Behaviour that is stalking, or that directly or indirectly harasses a person, or monitors or tracks a person's activities, communications or movements, whether by physically following the person, using technology or in another way.*
- *Behaviour that damages or destroys property.*
- *Behaviour that causes death or injury to an animal or otherwise makes use of an animal to threaten a person.*
- *Behaviour that prevents the second person from doing any of the following or otherwise isolates the person:*
  - *Making or keeping connections with the person's family, friends or culture.*
  - *Participating in cultural or spiritual ceremonies or practices.*
  - *Expressing the person's cultural identity.*
- *Behaviour that deprives the second person of liberty, restricts the second person's liberty or otherwise unreasonably controls or regulates a person's day-to-day activities.*
  - *Making unreasonable demands about how a person exercises the person's personal, social or sexual autonomy and making threats of negative consequences for failing to comply with the demands.*
  - *Denying a person access to basic necessities, including food, clothing or sleep.*
  - *Withholding necessary medical or other care, support, aids, equipment or essential support services from a person or compelling the person to take medication or undertake medical procedures.*

- *Domestic abuse includes behaviour by the first person that causes a child to hear or witness, or otherwise be exposed to the effects of, behaviour mentioned in subsection (1).*

Unfortunately, the first person to be arrested and charged under the new NSW Coercive Control laws, rather than being given a custodial sentence, was mandated to complete an 18-month intensive corrections order to be served in the community, wear an electronic ankle monitor and undertake 120 hours of community service. These kinds of sentencing decisions do not reflect the serious nature of coercive control and do not provide the victim-survivor with any sense of safety.

Of course, none of these laws assisted Emily. In the early 1990s, domestic violence was little understood, and the legislation was wholly inadequate.

Angharad Candlin

THREE

Emily grew up with a father who was focused on his work and on his numerous extramarital relationships. As was common in the 1970s and 1980s, particularly in Australia, the caring role was delegated to his wife. She was a social worker supporting complex families and was an expert in providing a safe and loving base for their daughters. I remember meeting her and observing how affectionate and demonstrative she was with her daughters. She was kind, loving and warmly accepted me. I felt like she was a person you could trust with your deepest secrets.

Emily's parents' relationship was far from happy. Emily recalls terrible arguments between them and times when she and her sister were locked out of the house due to the severity of the conflict. Her father regularly grabbed one of the kitchen knives and would threaten to harm or kill himself if his wife didn't stop whatever it was that he didn't like. At the first whiff of a fight, Emily and Susannah became adept at running into the kitchen, grabbing all the sharp knives and hiding them to prevent their father from using them.

As an adult, looking back on the relationship, it is clear to Emily that her father chose to use violence against his wife. The family had a shed in their back garden which Emily had furnished with cushions, blankets, drinks, snacks and changes of clothes for those times when the fights between her parents were prolonged. She and her sister took refuge there, and Emily tried to protect her younger sister from the impact.

Mary was diagnosed with brain cancer when Emily was 11. Emily remembers it clearly. Mary had three operations over the years to try and remove the tumours. As a young girl, Emily was confused and significantly impacted by her mother's ill health. Nobody really explained to the children what was happening. Fortunately, Mary did go into remission for a number of years, but as cancer so often does, it returned when Emily was about 17.

Emily was distraught about the possibility of losing her mother for a number of years before Mary actually died. Emily and her sister, Susannah, needed their mum. There were so many things that both girls needed that Mary couldn't provide due to her illness. Her premature death meant that these adolescent girls didn't have a mum when they needed her the most. Following Mary's death, my mum offered her support to Emily and Susannah, and whilst it was kind, it wasn't enough.

It is easy to look back and reflect on how her mum's death deeply impacted Emily. Not just in terms of her loss and grief but in terms of the wise counsel Mary could have offered to her daughter. I am confident that had Emily's mother not prematurely died, Emily would have had a very different life to the one she has. Instead, she was left with an emotionally remote father who really had no idea how to support two grieving daughters, essentially leaving them to their own devices. Rather than parent and care for his devastated children, he focussed on the children of the woman he had been having a relationship with. He didn't attend Emily or her sister's parents' evenings at school and, in the end, didn't attend Emily's university graduation.

Emily told the man who would become her abuser about her previous boyfriend, her father's behaviour and her overwhelming grief at the death of her mother. Her abuser took this information and used it to his advantage when grooming her. Perpetrators of violence often target women who are vulnerable. Emily was certainly vulnerable. She was also already somewhat isolated, particularly because she was attending university in a city different from her support network of friends. She was, for all intents and purposes, a sitting duck for a man who chose to control and abuse women.

There is too often a perception that women somehow choose men who perpetrate violence. There have been too many courses aimed at women to teach them about "*the cycle of violence*", exploring how they might, albeit subconsciously, invite violent men into their hearts and lives, how they need to change their thinking and behaviour. This is covert victim blaming at its worst. It implies that women choose violent men. There are no courses for men about not deliberately targeting women who are vulnerable.

Emily did not choose to have a relationship with a violent man. She fell in love with a man who was charming, affectionate and overtly loving. He then chose to terrorise and degrade her with surgical precision. The issue with blaming women for choosing violent men is that we get distracted by what women need to change. We miss the glaringly obvious issue that this man will then go on to perpetrate violence with more women unless he is challenged and supported to change.

He was the polar opposite of the other significant men in her life. Having been so isolated and disregarded, she was finally in a relationship with a man who treated her as if she were a precious jewel. He was a master of love bombing.

Once she returned to university for the new academic year, her boyfriend overwhelmed her with gifts, money, flowers and letters every other day. He told her how much he loved and adored her, how she was the only one for him. That he wanted to have babies with her and to grow old with her. He told her everything she had never been told before. This was a whole new experience, and as he had designed it, she fell in love with him. She felt valued by a man for the first time in her life.

Love bombing is also designed to confuse victim-survivors when the abuser becomes controlling and/or violent. When her boyfriend was first violent with Emily, she, like so many victim-survivors, was completely sideswiped by his behaviour because he had been so loving and demonstrative previously. It makes it easier for perpetrators to assert control because the victim-survivor believes the perpetrator when they apologise and explain the behaviour as a once-off.

Victim-survivors often initially feel concerned for the perpetrator because the behaviour came so entirely out of the blue. They worry that something must be happening they don't know about or that something they have done has triggered something in the perpetrator. Forgiveness and care in these circumstances come easily because victim-survivors love their partners deeply, as do any other couples. Emily did exactly that.

In return, he said that he didn't like her attending university in Canberra and wanted her to be in Sydney so that they could be together all the time, that he missed her deeply when she was away and wanted to just spend his time with her. Emily was, however, settled and enjoying her course. She had made a deliberate decision not to go to university in Sydney so that she could forge her own path away from her father. She was living independently, making new friends and enjoying the course. Quite reasonably, she told him she didn't want to change universities and return to Sydney and that seeing him when she returned to Sydney for a weekend or when he came down to Canberra would have to work until they both finished their degrees.

One Friday night, Emily went to a fairly typical university party with her flatmate Jen, and, as young students do, she and her friends got slightly drunk. Emily has a very slight frame and has always described herself as a bit of a lightweight when it comes to alcohol; one glass of wine will make her tipsy. A small group of the students, including Emily and Jen, ended up sitting outside the party on a grass verge, which the council had evidently just mowed, so there was loose grass everywhere.

The following morning, her boyfriend arrived as planned. For no reason whatsoever, he immediately inspected Emily's clothes and demanded to know why she had grass all over them. He came up very close and snarled that she wasn't allowed to go out without him and that she couldn't be trusted. Emily, shocked, decided at that point that she needed to curb her social life when he came to visit her in Canberra to avoid riling him up.

When I interviewed Emily for this book, I asked her why she stayed with him at that very early point in their relationship. She considered the question deeply and eventually responded because, the vast majority of the time, he was demonstratively caring, loving and attentive. His abusive behaviour seemed to be completely out of character. She also reflected that for the first nine months of their relationship, he was in Sydney, and she was in Canberra, so they weren't actually physically together the entire time.

He assaulted her on another occasion when he had come down to Canberra to visit her. By this time, he had become friendly with a number of Emily's friends and was comfortable being in social situations with them. On this particular occasion, they went to the University bar to meet some friends. Emily felt this was a low-risk situation because her boyfriend was fine with her socialising with her female friends, whom she would predominantly be talking to.

As expected, there were a number of Emily's friends and acquaintances at the bar, including a male student from her course who was clearly distressed about something. Emily is one of the kindest and most empathic people I know, and so, as is her character, she went and sat with him to try to offer him some support. Emily's boyfriend was close by the bar, talking to her friends. At any point, he could have approached Emily and her male friend and joined in the conversation with them. He chose not to. Instead, he glared at her across the tables. He was so aggressive in his looks that she felt she could do nothing but return to his side. After about 20 minutes, he hissed quietly at her that they needed to leave. Emily felt embarrassed and made her apologies to the group as they left.

He grabbed her elbow and forced her out of the bar. Once they were back at Emily's share house, he yelled at her and shoved her so hard she fell over. He shouted that she was making a spectacle of herself and berated her for showing him up, flaunting herself at other men when she was his girlfriend. He made it quite clear that she was to have absolutely no friendships with any males and have contact with them only in her lectures and only when she absolutely had to. This was a man who purported to love her deeply and passionately.

Emily found herself changing her behaviour around him. Whilst she had relative freedom because they were in different cities, she found herself keeping parts of her social life from him. It wasn't just her male friends that he had problems with. He not only criticised her female friends, but he also made increasingly derogatory comments about them. He also despised Emily's flatmate and close friend, Jen. Of course, he did this subtly, within the context of his continual love bombing of Emily.

He was deliberate in his behaviour. It is well known that the creators of Pokie Machines set them up so that users do have wins from time to time. It is the unpredictable wins that cause the user to continue gambling. Whilst Emily was in no way addicted or gambling with her perpetrator, the same neurochemical, dopamine, was activated by his behaviour. He would be charming and seem loving and attentive for the majority of the time, but then there would be a moment of aggression. Some might say it was because he loved Emily intensely. In fact, it was carefully calculated to control her.

Their "love affair" was around nine months old when Emily realised she was pregnant. Her boyfriend was overjoyed, and he took the opportunity to move down to Canberra so they could live together. Whilst he had been studying for a business degree, he left his course altogether so that he could be with her. His desire to control her, to own her, to abuse her surpassed even his own commitment to himself and his education now that she was pregnant with his child.

Emily moved out of her shared accommodation with her great-friend Jen, and she and her boyfriend moved in together. Whilst previously she had respite from his erratic behaviour, now he was living with her full time and permanently. He had failed to complete his university degree and had no job lined up. His lack of degree did not stop him from applying for jobs and falsifying applications stating that he had completed his Bachelor of Business Degree. Of course, Emily wasn't aware of this at the time; she was just relieved that he was successful in his application for a position with a local council as a Sports and Recreation Officer.

Gaslighting is a term often used in the context of domestic violence. It is drawn from the play Gaslight. The play was written in 1938 by Patrick Hamilton and set in 1880s London. The plot basically involves a husband carefully creating situations to confuse his wife and gradually send her mad so that he can access her wealth. Gaslighting is manipulating someone to convince them to doubt themselves and their reality.

Emily's abuser gaslighted her extensively throughout their marriage. He encouraged her, lovingly, of course, to leave her degree. He told her there was no way she could be a mother and a student. He undermined her by telling her it would be too much for her and that she would inevitably fail her degree. Surely, it was better to quit than to be seen as a failure. She didn't even need a degree because she would be at home with the children, and he would provide for them. She would have no need to work, and really, she wasn't that intelligent anyway, so why should she continue? He reminded her of things she had supposedly forgotten but that he had never actually spoken of. He moved items, so she thought she had lost them. He stalked her and then told her she was being hysterical and imagining things. Every purposeful step was designed to erode her confidence and sense of self. It worked.

He had disapproved of Emily's friends, and now he had the opportunity to control who she socialised with. He always had a plausible reason for her not to spend time with her friends. It always had to do with her looking after herself and the baby. She shouldn't go to the pub because people would be smoking and drinking around her, and that wasn't good for the baby or for her. She shouldn't go out for dinner with Jen and her other girlfriends because she needed to take it easy and put her feet up. He even insisted she had no reason to go to the library to study in the evenings because he could pick up whatever books she needed and bring them home so that she could study in the quiet of their small, one-bedroom apartment.

One of the hallmarks of coercive control is the isolation of the victim-survivor from their family and friends. These comments were designed to do just that. The more isolated Emily became, the more control he had over her. Spending less time with her friends meant that they were unlikely to see the abuse and intervene. Emily had become an expert at excusing or minimising his behaviour with her friends over the nine months of their relationship. As she battled to prevent his jealous outbursts, she found herself using her pregnancy as an excuse for not socialising with her friends.

Her friends were none the wiser; she was expecting a baby after all. Of course she was nauseous or tired. Of course she didn't want to spend time in the pub or stay up late.

Angharad Candlin

FOUR

Emily was increasingly bewildered by his behaviour. On one hand, he was demonstrative and loving, but on the other hand she felt uneasy about his subtle comments. Was she imagining it? He loved her so much. He couldn't possibly mean that she was so slow-witted or couldn't multi-task a degree course and care for a baby, especially given that he was so committed to being an involved dad. Nevertheless, that was how she was starting to feel.

In the very early stages of her pregnancy, Emily and I discussed the possibility of termination. Whilst my personal views generally lean against abortion for a host of reasons, I am fully committed to a woman's right to choose and to control her own body. Emily grappled deeply with her decision. She believed she was completely unprepared to become a mother. She felt overwhelmed by the idea of completing her degree whilst caring for an infant. Her grief at the death of her mother intensified with the pregnancy. Could she do this without her mum? Unbeknownst to me, she was also grappling with a boyfriend who was becoming increasingly abusive and controlling. She was fearful of what he might do if she did indeed terminate the pregnancy.

In the late 1980s and early 1990s, the phrase "coercive control" was not in our lexicon. If anyone did talk about domestic violence, it was, more often than not, mutualised and referred to as situational couple violence, meaning there was no primary aggressor; both had equal power in the relationship, and both parties were just as likely to perpetrate violence as each other.

Emily decided to go ahead with the pregnancy. She was rapidly heading towards her final year, and by the time the baby arrived, she would be nearing completion. She thought with her partner's help, she could just about do it. After all, he was doting towards their unborn baby and equally caring towards her.

Soon after his relocation to Canberra, he proposed. Emily wasn't particularly bothered about being married. She had seen how dysfunctional her parent's marriage had been, and marriage wasn't high on her list of priorities. Nevertheless, she accepted his proposal. They began planning a small wedding during the summer holidays.

During their engagement, Emily met his parents for the first time. She immediately warmed to his father but felt intimidated by his mother, whom she describes as highly controlling and cold. She wasn't at all comfortable with her future mother-in-law and felt like she was being scrutinised and judged as to whether she was good enough to marry into the family.

To the outside world, including myself, Emily seemed overjoyed and very much in love. In fact, privately, she was increasingly confused by his behaviour. He was loving and affectionate. He talked adoringly about them becoming a family, and he wanted at least four children. He whispered sweet things to the baby in her growing belly. He desired nothing more than to be a good father and husband. He reassured Emily she would be a wonderful mother.

It was during this time that I began to have some niggles about the man Emily was engaged to. She told me about an incident in the early stages of her pregnancy when she had "fallen" down the stairs. She was a little hazy on the details. My gut feeling wasn't good, but did I really think that a man could actually push or trip a woman - a woman pregnant with his child - down the stairs on purpose? I pushed aside my worries at the time, but if the same situation arose now, I would, without a shadow of a doubt, think that not only was it possible, but actually, it was probable. What I did do was tactfully express my concerns to Emily. She reassured me that things were ok. Now she asks herself why she didn't listen to me. She didn't listen because she was young and naive. She couldn't possibly imagine the future that has become her reality, and neither, to be honest, could I.

Emily doesn't recall this incident, mainly because it has merged with so many other incidents of abuse, but it has sat in the back of my mind for over three decades, more so now that I know the intimate details of the violence. I also now know the risk factors in relationships where violence occurs.

According to the Australian Institute of Health and Welfare[14];

- *1 in 7 women who experienced violence by a current partner and were pregnant during their relationship, experienced violence during their pregnancy.*

- *1 in 8 women experienced violence for the first time during pregnancy.*

- *46% of pregnant women assaulted by a partner in 2022-23 experienced injury to their trunk, compared to 29% of other women.*

Pregnancy is one of the most dangerous times for a woman when the man chooses to use coercive control.

Emily's wedding was organised for January 1989. I was once again in Sydney for Christmas and stayed until late January. I managed to fit the wedding in just prior to flying back to the UK. Emily invited me to her Hen's weekend events. She had planned a very civilised afternoon tea, followed by dinner and finally a visit to a local pub. When her fiancé heard about the plan, he insisted that he and his friends go to the same pub. Emily was annoyed by his decision; after all, it was her Hen's Party. She wanted to spend time with her girlfriends. Her expectation was that he would have a Bucks do with his friends, not combine the two. She didn't say anything for fear he would ruin her celebrations by becoming aggressive and controlling. Emily didn't tell us that her fiancé and his friends were going to be at the same pub we were going to. We arrived, and a short time later, the men arrived. We were not impressed. Emily's abuser was loud, jovial and drunk.

I had only briefly met the man Emily was to marry, but I was worried about him. This evening at the pub deepened those feelings. It is difficult to pinpoint exactly what it was about him that I reacted to. He was charming, confident and friendly. Was it because he had insisted he and his friends come to the same pub? Was it because he

---

14   https://www.aihw.gov.au/family-domestic-and-sexual-violence/population-groups/ pregnant-people 28th February 2025.

seemed to be just a touch patronising towards Emily and her female friends? Was it because he was slightly condescending towards the woman behind the bar and made a few mildly derogatory comments about some of the other women in the pub?

Ultimately, it was the way he treated Emily that garnered my strongest reaction. He intervened whenever she engaged in conversation with any of his male friends by leaving his conversation, coming up beside Emily and draping his arm around her. None of it "sat right" with me. Now, of course, I know he was exerting coercive control. Nothing was significant or obvious enough to draw attention to, but all of it, taken together, painted a picture.

The wedding took place the following weekend. Emily spent the night before her wedding with her father and sister. She recalls crying with them both and saying that she didn't want to get married. Emily felt trapped, and she didn't want her life to be controlled by someone else. She was 22 and wanted to be free to live her life without being answerable to anyone. Her father pressured her to go ahead with the wedding. She reluctantly agreed because she thought it would be better for her baby to have two parents and be raised in a stable family rather than by a single mum juggling work and parenting.

It was a small and intimate wedding held at Parramatta Registry Office. Both parents, siblings, Emily's grandmother and a few close friends attended. I was pleased to be invited. Emily was about six months pregnant, and she looked beautiful. She wore a pretty Laura Ashley dress with flowers in her long dark hair. The ceremony was simple and over quite quickly. Emily insisted that the only thing she really wanted at the wedding was confetti. As the couple left the building, we lined up on the street and threw confetti over them. We all walked to one of the local hotels for lunch in a private room. Emily's dad made a speech, as did Emily's new husband.

My negative feelings about the man Emily was marrying did not improve at the wedding. Again, I couldn't put my finger on what it was, but I had a physical reaction to him. Irrationally, I felt like I needed to take a shower after being around him. I couldn't ignore my gut feeling anymore, prompting me to walk over to him towards the end of the lunch. As I mentioned earlier, he was standing alone next to the cake table in the corner. The presents were all piled up on an adjacent table. I stood next to him and very quietly said that he would have to answer to me if he hurt Emily. Decades later, I still can't quite believe that I said it. I have never before or since done anything remotely similar. He looked at me silently, watching me as I walked away. Soon after, I said my goodbyes and left, but the nauseous feeling in the pit of my stomach remained.

I didn't have a lot of contact with Emily after her wedding. I was back at university in my final year, finishing off my dissertation and heading into final exam preparation. In July, however, I received a brief phone call from Emily, who told me she had given birth the previous day to a healthy baby boy, Ellis. When we spoke, she was on her own in the hospital. Her husband had not been in to visit her or the baby that day. She sounded nervous and quite alone.

When I asked her how the birth was, she told me that she had an epidural, but it had impacted her legs. She had gotten out of bed the night before to go to the toilet, and her legs gave way because she couldn't feel them. She was stuck in bed, reliant on the nurses, until the effect of the epidural wore off. Ellis was in a cot by her bed. During our phone call, she asked me a curious question: "*Can I hold him?*" I said he was her son, she could do whatever she liked with him, and she would be a brilliant mum.

I hung up the phone and was somewhat confused by her question. I wondered why she felt like she needed to ask. When Emily reflected on this decades later, she said that by this point, she felt so undermined by her new husband that she had lost all confidence in herself. He repeatedly told her that because she had no mother, she didn't know how to care for a baby. She didn't know how to be a parent. He told her that because her father was such a poor role model, she needed him to show her how a father is supposed to be.

When I saw her during my usual Christmas break, Emily told me later about the birth in more detail. She had gone into labour in the early hours of Saturday morning, so she woke her husband to let him know. He told her it was going to be hours and to try and get some more sleep, and then he fell back to sleep himself. They both got up the next day, and he carried on with his day as if nothing at all was different. Emily laboured at home alone without any support.

By the afternoon, her contractions were regular and growing in intensity. She told her husband and said she felt that they should go to the hospital. He was watching an international rugby match on television at the time, and he replied that they weren't going anywhere until the end of the game. Eventually, the match finished, and he drove her to the hospital. Her son was born very soon after their arrival. I was appalled, and the negative feelings I had about her husband escalated. I wanted to call him out for his selfishness but didn't want to upset Emily, so I remained silent.

Emily only had the mid-winter break to get used to being a mum before she had to quickly knuckle down and finish her degree. Fortunately, she only had a couple of lectures a week at this point in her course, and the university had a crèche that she made use of. Her husband was a doting father. The physical abuse that she had experienced prior to her marriage dissipated once Ellis was born.

Unusually, Emily had never learned to drive. Her mother had been ill when all of her friends were learning to drive, and she had no one to take her out to practice. Her father certainly didn't offer. This wasn't a particular issue in Sydney. Her family lived close to public transport links, so she was able to get around easily. In Canberra, it was harder. She discussed learning to drive with her husband, but he said no and that she really didn't need to because he could drive her wherever she needed to go, and he didn't think she'd be a very good driver anyway. She wasn't able to organise driving lessons herself because, as a student, she couldn't afford to pay for them, and once again, she had no one to take her out to practice. Just like her father, her husband wasn't going to assist her. Despite reassuring her that he could drive her to and from university, he rarely did. This left her to struggle alone on the buses with a young baby, a pram and her university books. His disparaging remarks about her capacity to drive eroded her self-confidence even more, and she became convinced she would be a terrible driver.

FIVE

Once Emily finished her degree, the little family moved back to Sydney from Canberra. Emily stayed at home with Ellis whilst her husband had been successful in his job application to another local council, this time as a Manager of Sports and Recreation. The initial falsification of his degree was no longer relevant. His previous experience with a local council in Canberra, along with a positive reference, was apparently enough to satisfy the recruitment requirements.

Emily and I continued to write to each other, and at the end of 1990, I permanently migrated to Sydney. I was delighted to have a ready-made friend whilst I found my feet. I had a new job and lots of friends from the UK came to stay with me in my first couple of years. Emily had a new baby, so I was pleased to catch up with her when we could both fit it in. She was incredibly happy to be a mum, and she clearly adored her son. Her grandmother came to stay quite often, and she caught up with her long-standing school friends. Her husband was enjoying being a father. I assumed their relationship was fine.

About 18 months after Ellis' birth, Emily had baby number two, a girl named Hannah. Another 18 months later, she had a boy called Patrick and 15 months later, another boy, Hugh. She had four children under five by the time she was 27. When I asked Emily how her relationship was when she had her children, she told me that her husband had not been violent whilst she was having babies, but he was still controlling.

While Emily was in the baby phase with her first three children, she decided that she wanted to become a teacher and applied to the local College of Advanced Education to do a one-year postgraduate certificate in teaching. She was successful in her application; however, she found herself pregnant with her fourth child, so she deferred the course for 12 months.

Emily was delighted to welcome her new baby, Hugh. She was still committed to becoming a teacher. However, her husband discouraged her. He was disparaging of her capacity to teach. He insisted there was no way she could study and mother four children at the same time, despite the fact that she had a baby during her degree and successfully graduated. The debate about her ongoing study was arduous and prolonged. Eventually, her abuser decided that if he was going to have a successful career - which would mean relocating as he worked his way up the ladder - having a wife with transferable skills would probably be quite handy and of financial benefit. It was never about Emily being fulfilled.

Finally, he relented, and she took up her teacher training place when Hugh was about nine months old. She organised through her sister, a student nursery teacher, to care for Patrick and Hugh during the day while Ellis and Hannah were at preschool. The student teacher would pick the older children up, have them settled at home and leave when Emily returned from college.

Emily was also worried about her grandmother, who was clearly getting older and a little more frail. She managed to persuade her husband to let her grandmother move in with them so that she could care for her. She moved in about two months after Hugh was born.

Emily's husband rarely took responsibility for the care of the children and usually worked late. Despite having agreed for her to study, he clearly did not like her being away from him and the children. He would show up unannounced, wait for the lecture to finish and then take her home. He would question who she was socialising with at college. He made it very clear that she was not to sit with or spend any time with the male students.

There were two occasions where Emily was really surprised by her husband's reactions to what she thought were fairly innocuous events. The first related to her attendance at a one-day assertiveness course at the local community centre. He was livid with her when he found out she had been. The second was related to her attendance at an evening at her college where a hypnotist was "performing". Her husband was away with work. When he returned, she told him about it. She and her friends thought it was quite a fun evening. On the other hand, he railed at her for going, saying she could have been hypnotised without knowing and could have said anything.

Emily and I discussed them both years later. We both came to the conclusion that the idea of her learning to be assertive could have threatened his control of her. As for the hypnotist, we both thought it was ridiculous that he had an issue with it. Still, on reflection, we decided that it was highly likely he was afraid she could have unknowingly disclosed the relentless abuse he was perpetrating.

One evening, a dinner was organised for the students and their partners. Emily and her husband attended. Everyone was sitting at a long table; Emily's husband was sitting opposite her, and a male student sat between Emily and his wife. It was a lovely evening where the students and their partners got to know each other. Conversations about their studies, lives, experiences and so forth were shared. At the end of the dinner, unexpectedly, Emily's husband took her to one side and said they needed to go home because she had "*shown him up*".

She was taken aback by this. After all, he had been sitting right opposite her. He had joined in the conversations with the people around them at the table. As they left the restaurant and moved out of sight of the windows, he twisted Emily's arm up her back with one hand and grabbed her hair with the other, pulling her head back and hissing that she had been fondling the man sitting next to her. Emily was terrified. The restaurant wasn't far from their home, so they had chosen to walk. Her husband marched her home, holding onto her hair and pinning her arm behind her and all the time berating her for showing him up and fondling the other man under the table. She had no idea if anyone witnessed this event. If they did, unsurprisingly, they didn't intervene or say anything.

Once home, his violence increased. He silently and, with great force, shoved her forward. As she stumbled and fell, he kicked her down the stairs. As she lay on the ground at the bottom of the stairs, he sat on top of her and strangled her. She passed out. This was, by far, the worst violence Emily had experienced to date, and she was now terrified of her husband. When Emily described it to me, I instantly recalled the story she had told me about falling down the stairs during her first pregnancy. I was both outraged and distraught by this story. Distraught that this man had attempted to murder my lovely friend. Distraught that she had kept it secret for so many years.

During this period in her life, there was a second incident of attempted murder. Again, it followed a night out with her student friends to a local pub. He was, as usual, with her. She wasn't allowed to have any social life without him. Following the evening, he once again marched her home, yanking her hair. When they got home, he shouted furiously at her for flirting with the male students, grabbed a plastic shopping bag and held it over her head. He released her just before she lost consciousness.

I couldn't believe that Emily hadn't told me about these incidents previously. My poor friend had been living in hell, keeping her husband's violence a secret. I knew their marriage wasn't great, but I had no idea just how bad it was. Even having written this book with Emily, I'm still trying to process it.

In New South Wales, there is now an assessment tool used by government and non-government services who work with victim-survivors of domestic violence called the Domestic Violence Safety Assessment Tool, commonly known as the DVSAT[15]. It is designed specifically to be used with victim-survivors of intimate partner violence. It is a questionnaire with 25 questions for the victim-survivor and a section for the assessor to complete regarding their "Professional Judgement". The answers are multiple choice: Yes, No, Don't Know, Refused to Answer. If a victim-survivor answers yes to any of the questions, they are considered to be "at threat". If they answer yes to 12 or more questions, they are considered to be at "serious threat". If someone is at "serious threat", there is a system in place to ensure that these victim-survivors do not fall through the cracks and receive services and support as quickly as possible.

The third question on the list is, *"Has your partner ever choked, strangled, suffocated you or attempted to do any of these things?"*

---

15 https://www.facs.nsw.gov.au/__data/assets/file/0010/592948/ DVSAT.pdf

Whilst all of the questions on the DVSAT relate to extremely serious incidents, this question is an immediate red flag to those who work in the sector.

In 2018, a suite of amendments were passed as part of the NSW Crimes Legislation Amendment Bill[16]. Within this bill was the new crime of Intentional Strangulation. According to the latest NSW Domestic Violence Death Review Report 2021-2023;[17] *"The second most common manner of homicide was suffocation/strangulation".* Glass et al[18] state *"The odds of becoming a victim of attempted homicide increased by about seven-fold for women who had been strangled by their partner".*

If there had been any question in Emily's mind previously, there were absolutely no doubts now that her husband could be a very dangerous and abusive man. She was terrified of him.

While the family was living in Sydney, they were invited to the wedding of a work colleague of Emily's husband. They went along to the celebrations, with Emily thinking nothing of it. Decades later, her abuser told her sneeringly that he had been having an affair with the woman at the time of her wedding. He also told her about the countless affairs and women he had sex with throughout the 26 years of their marriage.

Emily told me about an incident that happened some years after her divorce. She was at a restaurant with a friend. On the next table, she overheard a couple talking about some people Emily knew from her time living in Tasmania. She interrupted them to let them know about their mutual acquaintances. The woman had worked at the same place as Emily's ex-husband. They talked about all of the other people they both knew. Emily dropped the name of her ex-husband. The woman raised her eyebrows and said he had a reputation for taking any new interns under his wing, having sex with them and then passing them off to other colleagues. He had a reputation for his multiple affairs. Clearly, women to him were just an object for his

---

16 https://legislation.nsw.gov.au/view/pdf/asmade/act-2018-83 Page 9

17 https://www.nsw.gov.au/sites/default/files/noindex/2024-08/domestic-violence-death-report.pdf Page 51

18 Non Fatal Strangulation is an important risk factor for homicide of women. Journal of Emergency Medicine 35, p 329 2008

own gratification. He had no qualms about breaking social norms and ethical behaviour if it meant satisfying himself.

Interestingly, the very behaviour he consistently accused Emily of was the behaviour he was engaged in. Telling Emily about his sexual partners was designed to humiliate and degrade her. I also wonder about the wellbeing of the multiple other women he has used, particularly the young interns.

I want to draw the reader's attention to the concept of "*relationship*" when violence is used. We often hear the term "*abusive relationship*" or "*domestic violence relationship*". Where violence is used, there is no relationship. Even if the couple have been married or de facto for decades. If one person is perpetrating violence against their partner, it is not a relationship. We need to be very careful about the language we use when describing domestic violence. Rather than "*abusive relationships*" or similar, we need to change our language to "*x has a history of perpetrating violence against y*". The status of any "relationship" is irrelevant when it comes to violence.

When we use the term abusive relationship, there is also no information about who the perpetrator is. It mutualises the situation, and it infers that it is situational couple violence, that both are at fault. When we use the sentence, "*x has a history of perpetrating violence against y,*" we are being clear about the perpetrator and the victim.

We also need to be careful about how our sentences are framed. We often start with "*y is a victim of domestic violence*". When we say this, we lose sight of the perpetrator. Most recently, the world has been horrified at the mass rape trial held in France. What we have seen over and over again are the words "*Gisele Pelicot rape trial*". It actually wasn't Gisele Pelicot's rape trial, it was Dominique Pelicot's and the 52 other men's rape trial; Gisele Pelicot was a witness. When we don't mention the perpetrator's name, they aren't held to account. We don't even know the names of the other perpetrators unless we look carefully.

Despite guidelines for the reporting of domestic violence, we all too frequently see careless media reporting with headlines such as; "*sport star x's wife assaulted*". What headlines do in these situations is erase the victim and fail to hold the perpetrator to account. We don't know her name and don't know who the perpetrator of the violence is. When we use language such as "*sports star x found guilty of a history and pattern of domestic violence perpetrated against his partner y*", it is clear who the perpetrator is and who the victim is. It is also clear that there is a history of violence, which counteracts the common rhetoric that the perpetrator just "snapped", that it was "just" one incident.

Often people make a decision not to use the name of the perpetrator. This may be to protect the safety of the victim, or so that the perpetrator doesn't have the satisfaction of becoming well known and their cause normalised or even celebrated. The New Zealand Prime Minister, Jacinda Ardern, publicly announced that she would not use the name of the perpetrator of the 2019 Christ Church Mosque shooting in order that he not gain the satisfaction of public notoriety. These carefully chosen situations are entirely different to the indifferent and inaccurate way domestic violence is reported in the media. All media must improve the way they report domestic violence, particularly the attention-grabbing headlines.

Angharad Candlin

SIX

When Emily's children were still very young, she was shocked one day when two practitioners from the child protection department arrived at her doorstep. They told her that they had received a report that she had sexually abused her little boys. Emily was horrified. She would never abuse a child. She was a newly graduated teacher. What could this mean? When she spoke to her husband about it, he confirmed that he had made the report. Of course, a child protection investigation ensued. She was interviewed, and the children were interviewed. Her sons were as confused as she was and denied that mummy had done anything remotely inappropriate. The child protection team were completely satisfied that no abuse had occurred, and in due time, the case was closed. What the child protection department didn't do was question why the father of the children would make a report about the safety of his own children. He was never investigated and never held to account for this false allegation.

There are many assertions about false allegations, particularly in child custody disputes. Many male support groups regularly claim that there are large volumes of cases where men have been falsely accused of sexually or physically abusing their children. False allegations are a vexing issue. More research is certainly needed about this specific area. Most of the data indicates that vexatious complaints of child abuse generally are very low (less than 5%); however, Trocme and Bala[19] specifically investigated false allegations in custody disputes.

---

19 Trocme and Bala "False Allegations of abuse and neglect when parents separate" in Child Abuse and Neglect; 2005 Dec. 29(12):1333-45.

Their findings, despite the consistent assertion that women make the largest number of false allegations, demonstrate that "... *noncustodial parents (usually) fathers most frequently make intentionally false reports. Of the intentionally false allegations of maltreatment tracked by the CIS-98, custodial parents (usually mothers) and children were least likely to fabricate reports of abuse and neglect.*" Their research indicates that 2% of custodial parents (generally mothers) and 15% of non-custodial parents (generally fathers) make vexatious complaints. Only 4% of all child protection reports are considered to be intentionally fabricated. Of that 4%, 12% occurred in a custody or access dispute.

It is important to clarify that there is a significant difference between unsubstantiated reports and intentionally fabricated or vexatious reports. According to Trocme and Bala and numerous other evidence-based reports, about 33% of all maltreatment investigations are unsubstantiated, meaning not enough evidence was available to prove abuse or neglect occurred.

In Australia, we are fortunate to have a system that works alongside the Family Court in partnership with the various state Child Protection Departments: the Magellan List. The Magellan program offers specialist casework support and assessment where child protection reports have been made. Additional court resources are put in place to move the matter through the legal system in a more timely fashion.

The pervasive narrative that women make false reports to prevent fathers from having contact with their children is erroneous, and it needs to stop. When anyone - male/female/child/adult - makes false allegations, actual victim-survivors become even more unsafe because they are less likely to be believed. Like the allegations of women being violent, yes, some women are violent, but almost all violence is perpetrated by men. Yes, some women make false allegations about child abuse, but the vast majority of false allegations are made by men.

I don't doubt that in men's support groups, some men are victim-survivors of domestic violence, and some men have had false allegations made about them. I have worked with these men and know how devastating it can be. There are a number of issues, however, that must be acknowledged.

1. The levels of domestic violence are catastrophic. There will be many male victim-survivors, and there will be many who are falsely accused simply because the numbers around domestic violence are enormous. It may seem to participants in these men's groups that the numbers of male victim-survivors are large. Still, when you look at the number as a percentage, it is a tiny fraction of the violence and false allegations perpetrated by men against women.

2. When a minority of men discount the experiences of women because "*men are victims too,*" it polarises the community, which ultimately makes all victim-survivors more unsafe. Actually, what we should be saying is: ALL violence is unacceptable irrespective of who the victim-survivors are, AND we recognise the fact that women are the largest victim group of domestic violence, AND men are the largest victim group of generalised violence, AND the vast majority of violence is perpetrated by men, irrespective of the gender of the victim, AND all women are murdered by men, AND almost all men are murdered by men. Rather than dismissing the call of the community to keep women safe because "*men are victims too*", I suggest it would be more helpful for them to join in solidarity with women to address male violence.

3. Not all men who attend men's support groups are victim-survivors. Some present themselves as victim-survivors, but we know that men who use coercive control are experts at disguising their abuse. This is an uncomfortable truth, but it is one that has to be addressed. Volunteer male support group facilitators are experienced, kind and well-meaning: good men who want to make a difference. They are to be commended. Generally speaking, though, they do not have rigorous and specialised training in domestic violence and coercive control. Respectfully and without judgment, when group facilitators are not trained, they do not know what to look for, and they are not experts in pre-group screening.

What the government needs to do is fund specialised training and clinical supervision for male support group facilitators so that they can be far more effective in their support of genuine male victim-survivors.

4. Men don't come forward and identify themselves as victim-survivors. No, they don't, but neither do women. In fact, I would argue that because of the appalling way women victims of sexual and domestic violence have been and still are treated within the criminal court system, the way mothers have been and still are demonised within the family court system and the way women have been and still are blamed within the children's court system, far fewer women identify themselves as victim-survivors. They know it will not end well for either themselves or their children, so they keep quiet.

When Hugh was a toddler, Emily's husband decided that it was time for the family to move to Tasmania to be close to his family. Without consulting Emily, he had successfully applied once again for a management position in local government. He reasoned that with four children, it would be financially beneficial to buy a house, something they would not have been able to do in Sydney. Emily was distraught at the prospect of moving away, but he wouldn't listen to any of her reasons for staying in Sydney. Her sister was away at university herself by now, but her father, who had since married again, was still in Sydney, as were her long-term friends, including me and her grandmother. She would also be further away from her dear university friend, Jen, who had stayed in Canberra.

They stayed with Emily's parents-in-law for a few months until they found a suitable house. Emily adored her father-in-law. He was gentle and kind, the complete opposite of his wife. He took a great interest in Emily and the children and had plenty of time because he was retired. He loved talking to Emily about history and literature. Her husband started working soon after they arrived, so Emily and the children had plenty of time to settle in and get used to the much slower pace of Tasmania.

The close living arrangements meant that Emily's parents-in-law could see how their son was treating Emily. Her father-in-law expressed his concerns to her. Despite Emily's mother-in-law's relatively cold demeanour, she also observed the way her son was treating his wife. Along with her husband, she told him in no uncertain terms that his behaviour was unacceptable. He completely ignored his parents' admonishment.

Emily loved the house they moved into. It was an old Federation house with a large open plan area attached by a glassed-in walkway. They engaged builders and transformed this part of the house into a granny flat for Emily's grandmother. She had sold her home and added it to the finances needed to purchase the house. The house needed a complete renovation to the bathrooms and kitchen. Emily and her husband started the building work with gusto. He was quite practical, so he spent most weekends doing as much of the renovation as possible. Emily has always had an eye for colour and interior design, so she spent her time making curtains, looking for paint colours, and fossicking in op shops, garage sales, and builders' yards for interesting pieces to decorate the house.

Despite the profound violence, coercive control and gaslighting that Emily's husband perpetrated, he was always kind to Emily's grandmother. He seemed to care about her genuinely and went out of his way to help her with anything. Emily's grandmother was oblivious to the abuse. She was in a separate part of the house and didn't engage in the hustle and bustle of family life. She knew her grandson-in-law was "shouty", but she had no idea what was truly happening. Nevertheless, like me, she had a sense that he was not a good man, and although she disguised it, she disliked him intensely.

I was busy with work, and given my schedule, limited holiday time and the cost of flights, I didn't visit until January prior to Ellis starting school. I too, loved the house, but I was worried that they were quite isolated and Emily had never learned to drive. There was a bus to the nearest town twice a day, but that was it. This was before the days of Uber, and taxis were few and far between. I had hired a car, so for the week that I stayed, Emily, myself and the children took time to explore a bit further afield.

One evening, whilst Emily was bathing the younger children, her husband, Ellis, and I were in the lounge room. We were talking to Ellis about starting school in February. Ellis' father put his hands into fists and held them up like a boxer. He told Ellis that if any child bullied him, he should punch him. As he did this, he jabbed in the air towards Ellis. He asked Ellis to make fists and show him how he could punch people.

I was appalled. By now, I was studying for my Masters Degree, part-way through my Psychologist registration and working full-time alongside the Foster Care and Child Protection system. I couldn't maintain my silence. I interjected and firmly said, "*No, Ellis, if another child bullies you, you need to tell a teacher or one of the other adults at school. It's not ok to punch people.*" As I said this, I looked at Ellis' father with a very firm expression. I was expecting him to respond by telling me to mind my own business, but he didn't.

Later on, I told Emily about the exchange. She thanked me for intervening and said that her husband was furious but that he was also "*scared*" of me. I was surprised by this. I didn't think he was scared of anyone. I asked Emily why he felt that way. She said it was because he knew I was completely uncompromising, that he couldn't manipulate me and knew I wouldn't tolerate any kind of poor behaviour. He was right. He also used to stay well clear of me when I was visiting. I thought that this was out of respect for my friendship with Emily and that he wanted to give us time together. Now, I believe it was because he thought I would be able to see right through him and challenge him about his abuse.

SEVEN

Emily had qualified as a teacher and wanted to find a job. Her husband tried to dissuade her. As usual, he undermined her capacity to do the job. He told her she was too ineffective to manage a classroom full of children, and she had small children at home who needed her to parent them full-time. Emily, however, remained committed to her desire to be a teacher despite his gaslighting.

Her first job happened to be at the school Ellis was attending, so she could be near him during the day. However, the practical issue to overcome was that she still couldn't drive. She needed her husband to drive the whole family into town to drop the younger children off at daycare and pre-school, followed by her and Ellis at the local primary school. He did this reluctantly and with a significant amount of complaining and emotional abuse. He was often away with work, which would leave Emily to get all four children on the early bus into town, do all the drop-offs and then pick them all up to get the one bus back to their home at the end of the day. It was exhausting, but she was determined.

Abusers who use coercive control work hard to isolate their victims. He had managed to isolate Emily from her university friends. He had insisted they move to Tasmania, so he successfully isolated her from her long-term school friends and family. He didn't count Emily's grandmother because she was elderly; in his eyes, she was irrelevant and had no power or influence over his wife. He had also isolated her from me, the one person he was apparently scared of. The one person who he knew would have stood up to him and moved heaven and earth to remove Emily and her children from his abuse.

He had a vested interest in ensuring I couldn't be in regular contact with Emily as I had been when we were both in Sydney.

He also kept her isolated from making new friends and connections in Tasmania by refusing to let her get a driving license. As much as he hated having to drive Emily and the children, he hated the idea of her independence even more. Emily used the opportunity of her husband regularly travelling for work to learn how to drive secretly. She saved money from her salary to pay for regular lessons, fitting in as many as she could when he was away and then having a break when he was back. Eventually, she was ready to take her test, which she passed the first time. She had also secretly been saving to purchase a car. Finally, she had some level of freedom and independence.

He was furious that she had learned to drive behind his back and that she had used "*their*" money to pay for lessons and buy a car. As usual, he belittled her and told her she couldn't possibly be competent enough to drive and would be a danger to their children and the other drivers on the road. He continued to gaslight her, stripping away her self-esteem, expressed his disgust with her and continued to abuse and assault her at every opportunity.

I could never understand why Emily had never learned to drive. I appreciated how difficult it was when her mother was ill, but there was absolutely no reason for not learning when she was older. I had no idea that it was her husband's interference and gaslighting that had stopped her. She never articulated to me that there were any issues other than she didn't really feel driving was important, and that the family were well served by public transport. When I visited for the first time, I realised how isolated the family were and was confused by Emily's assertion that they were well-serviced by public transport. I completely missed the opportunity to be curious about this situation and didn't question her any further. I wished I had.

One day, on a whim, Emily decided to have her belly button pierced. A few days later, she was hanging out the washing while the children were playing in the garden. As she reached up, her newly pierced navel was momentarily visible. Her husband saw it and immediately pointed it out with disgust in his voice. He told her she was a "*disgusting whore*" whilst he aggressively escorted her into the house. He retrieved his pliers from his tool kit, and in direct view of the full-length kitchen windows, he pushed her to the floor, sat on top of her and wrenched the piece of jewellery out. The children were only metres away in the garden, and if they had turned around, they would have seen what their father was doing. Perhaps they did see it, but they never mentioned anything. Emily managed to breathe through the pain and not cry out so as not to alert the children. Unsurprisingly, her belly button became infected, required regular wound care, and she had to take a course of antibiotics.

His abusive behaviour included sexual violence. In the early 1990s, the concept of rape within marriage was not generally understood or talked about. There was still this notion, in many quarters, that men had a "right" to sexual intercourse whenever they felt like it if they were married. That the marriage contract was, in fact, a contract about sex. It remains the view in many faith communities. Indeed, even Emily herself didn't understand at the time that his behaviour was sexual violence. She thought it was just about having sex that she didn't want or enjoy.

Emily's perpetrator would stand in front of the full-length mirror in their bedroom and make her watch whilst he masturbated, admiring his reflection. He would proudly talk about his "*stiffy*". Once he had finished, he would have sex with Emily. In the early stages of their marriage, he would also declare loudly and proudly that he was going to "*impregnate*" her. Sex was never about her. Having children was never a decision she was part of. It was always about his own pleasure. Some may view this behaviour as odd or perhaps even a sex game. It is, in fact, abuse; there was no consent. She had no choice in this situation other than to watch him. He wouldn't let her leave, and she was afraid that if she did, he would beat her. She was afraid that if he beat her, the children would hear. She suffered in silence, protecting her children and herself.

As her marriage continued, the sexual violence she endured escalated. On many occasions, he would tie her hands together over her head as he raped her repeatedly in many different and humiliating ways; orally, anally, degrading her and insulting her as he did so. This was her husband, and he treated her like a piece of meat. There was no respect, no care, no love. She was just a way for him to satisfy his own perverse pleasure.

His sexual abuse of Emily could also be very subtle. Emily recalled an occasion when her father was visiting them. Emily, her husband and her father were having a drink in the garden. Her husband sat next to her, draped his arm around her shoulder and moved his hand inside her top, cradling her breast, whilst he continued the conversation as if this was a perfectly normal thing to do with his wife in front of his father-in-law, Emily was humiliated, and her father embarrassed. He and Emily talked about it later on, and her father surmised that the action was intended to taunt him. It was just another form of coercive control, and yet her father didn't take his son-in-law aside and chastise him or even have a quiet conversation about respect. He turned his head away and, once again, let his daughter down.

Returning to the trial of Dominique Pelicot and his co-accused, Gisele Pelicot waived her right to anonymity to ensure that the names of the perpetrators were released and that the legal fraternity and the community at large understood clearly that a woman not saying no is not consent. Further, everyone would be very clear that perpetrators of violence are normal, everyday people. Going about their lives just like everyone else. These men were married, single, middle class, working class, older and younger. An abuser is much more likely to be the person sharing your bed or the person next door than a stereotypical caricature of a violent man.

Emily's husband needed to maintain the facade of a "good" family man. How could he justify his teacher wife not being able to drive or be independent if anyone were to ask questions? It simply wouldn't add up to the image he was focused on portraying. Allowing her to drive also meant he wouldn't have to take the time or go out of his way to drop off the children and his wife or pick them up after work to take them home. It meant that he could stay late at work - although, as Emily later discovered, it was actually because he was having multiple affairs. On this occasion, he conceded his position in the conflict about Emily's driving.

I visited the family a few times whilst they were living in this house before Emily passed her driving test. Every time I visited, Emily knew what time my flight was coming in. She knew that I would hire a car and drive to them and that I would be with them about an hour and a half after I landed. Each time, her husband made sure that the family weren't home. My visits were inevitably during the school holidays or on long weekends. Her husband would surprise the family with a camping trip. Knowing full well what time I was arriving, he would ensure they didn't come home until a few hours later. It was his way of covertly exerting control over me, the woman who had seen through his facade at the earliest stage and called him out for what he was: an abusive man. At the time, I just thought he was being a tosser and decided that engaging with him would just play into his childish behaviour, so I ignored it. Now, knowing what was actually going on, I am frustrated with myself for not addressing it. Again, how I wish I had done things differently.

The first time it happened, I was irritated, but given that Emily's grandmother was at home, I had a cup of tea with her, and we caught up while we waited for them to arrive home. They were about half an hour late. Of course, he gave a plausible explanation for their late arrival; there was traffic, and he needed to get petrol. On every subsequent occasion that I visited, the period of time I was made to wait for their arrival increased. There was always a reason, and Emily was always the one to apologise. It wasn't necessary. I would spend the time waiting for the family's return with Emily's grandmother, whom I loved dearly. It was very clear to me that she intensely disliked her granddaughter's husband.

The last time I visited them in this house, her husband, unusually, went out of his way to be friendly. He, Emily and I all made dinner together, listening and singing to a 1980s playlist. Dinner was enjoyable and relaxed. He opened some wine and drank the majority of the bottle. Emily didn't really drink very much and had a glass, perhaps two. I'm allergic to wine and rarely drink, so I had a single gin and tonic. The following day, he took Emily, Ellis and me out in his 4WD up and down tracks in the bush. It was a fun afternoon. I found myself softening to him. Thinking perhaps he was improving. I was wrong. Now that I know what was actually going on, I feel disgusted that he played me into considering the concept that he might have been an okay person. When I remember it, I feel like I need to take a shower to wash him off me.

Emily and I had some time alone together during the weekend, and she asked me if I was happy. We ended up having a long conversation about the differences between happiness and joy. Emily spoke at length about the joy she felt with her children. She expressed her frustration that she didn't have more independence and freedom. I failed to notice what went unsaid. Her comments were indirect and so subtle that I completely missed the subtext. My career was also more focused on the wellbeing of children at the time, so whilst I understood domestic violence, I certainly didn't appreciate the complex nuances of coercive control or the damage it does to children.

I didn't have much contact with Emily in the years following this visit. I was completely swamped juggling the finalisation of my Masters, the requirements of my psychologist registration, transitioning into my first management role, supervising my team and dealing with the enormous caseload we had.

Emily had finally passed her driving test and was ensconced in her role as a teacher and mum to four primary-aged children. She also had a husband who apparently worked long hours and travelled a lot for his work. Her grandmother also sadly died, which meant Emily no longer had an ally or someone to help her with the children.

Emily, however, loved her time with the children when her husband was absent. She made sure that the time they had together was special, and she focussed on them entirely. She taught in the same school they attended, so in contrast to the traumatic periods when her husband was home, they regularly had times of peace and meaningful connection. As her daughter matured, they went away annually for a week together to explore historical sites or places of literary significance. Despite the abuse from her husband and his endless attempts to undermine her parenting, she focused on ways she could build her relationship with each of her children, individually and together.

In contrast to Emily, her husband was not an involved father. He was regularly absent. He didn't attend any of his children's school concerts or parent-teacher interviews or help with their homework. He attended their sporting events and took them "adventuring", such as 4 Wheel Driving or camping. They were things he wanted to do, to which the children were invited, rather than engaging with the children's pursuits.

EIGHT

About ten years after Emily and her husband were married, a close friend got married. Emily and her husband attended the wedding. There is a photo on Emily's mantelpiece of her the morning of the wedding. She looks absolutely beautiful. It was the day when her life changed profoundly.

Some months earlier, Emily and her husband had decided to try and improve their relationship by enrolling in Salsa classes, which they both enjoyed. It was a rare period of respite when their relationship was reasonable. They took the opportunity of the wedding to practice their newly acquired dancing skills.

The bride and groom had a beautiful wedding at an old heritage-listed property. Towards the end of the reception, Emily and her husband were dancing enthusiastically; unfortunately, someone had spilled a drink on the floor. As Emily spun around, the move became a trifle more dramatic than she intended. She slipped into the puddle. As she fell, she smacked her head on the corner of the marble table holding the wedding cake. Her head hit the floor, rebounded up then down, and she hit her chin. There was blood pouring out of her head everywhere. Emily's children were all at the wedding and saw the accident. Ellis ran over to her, sat on the floor and held her hand, trying to comfort her, clearly terrified. Several medically trained guests at the wedding rushed to Emily's assistance, and someone called for an ambulance.

The paramedics rapidly assessed Emily and drove at speed to the nearest hospital. She slipped into a coma for three or four days and spent weeks in hospital recovering. Once she regained consciousness, she and her husband were told that she almost died from the brain injury she received. Her husband listened silently.

The newlyweds were naturally mortified by what had happened. They postponed their honeymoon to care for Emily's children until she was discharged. Her husband was quite rattled by this event and was told by the medical staff that they didn't know what the long-term impact of the head injury would be.

The first time he brought the children, all aged under 11, into the hospital, Emily was devastated to find she couldn't remember their names. She recalls the children, particularly Ellis, looking confused and overwhelmed. They weren't able to comprehend what had happened to their mother, not understanding why she couldn't remember things or speak properly.

Emily had acquired a significant brain injury, which required about 12 months of intensive rehabilitation. Her short-term memory was impacted, as was her receptive and productive language. Initially, she experienced chronic confusion. As a result of the therapy she received, she slowly recovered. During this time, after his initial concern, her husband took every opportunity to insult, demean, gaslight, and, in a very calculated way, strip away any self-esteem she had left. He repeatedly told her she was an embarrassment, disgusting, that she was a useless mother, that she couldn't possibly work again, and that she should be ashamed to be seen in public because she was so ugly.

Emily recalls with crystal clarity the words he continually spat at her. After three decades in practice, I have become an expert in assessment. During the interviews I had with Emily for this book, it was patently obvious when she was directly quoting the insults he bathed her in. The power of his words remains palpable.

Despite the head injury and ongoing occupational therapy, after about six months, Emily was desperate to go back to teaching. Her Principal was incredibly supportive and agreed for her to start back gradually. Her allied health team would have preferred that she stay off work for some more time, but they supported her decision.

She continued her therapy around her work schedule. After a further six months, her specialists gave her a clean bill of health, permission to drive again and to basically continue living her life without any ongoing medical intervention. I spoke to Emily on numerous occasions during this time, and through our conversations, I could clearly perceive the gradual improvements she was making. Initially, I could hear how badly her speech was impacted, but over the course of that year, it continually developed until I couldn't detect any abnormalities.

Emily's husband, however, had a vested interest in Emily continuing to be disabled. He regularly and consistently pointed out all of her impairments, most of them fabricated. He ignored the medical approval she had been given to drive and railed at her at every opportunity, insisting that she couldn't drive, she wasn't safe behind the wheel of a car and would put her children and the other road users at risk. Having an injured wife simply played into the false narrative he was presenting to the rest of the world as a supportive husband and father juggling a stressful and difficult experience.

Nevertheless, Emily held her ground, and once he left the house in the mornings, she resisted his abuse and drove her car. It is a testament to Emily's resilience that she came through this period of time. Indeed, her resilience is remarkable, given her husband's endless gaslighting and grinding down of her self-esteem. Emily was focused on being the best mum and teacher she could be. She refused to let her husband take those things from her.

Whilst the abuse rained upon Emily started very early in their relationship, the accident and head injury seemed to be a catalyst for her husband to further escalate his violence and coercive control. He took every opportunity to gaslight, insult, assault and control her. Returning to work meant she could be with her children during the day. She could be around supportive friends and colleagues. She could continue earning money so that she had a level of independence. She could hear an alternative narrative than the one he consistently hurled at her. A narrative that built her up instead of tearing her down.

Victim-survivors of domestic violence resist the abuse in a variety of different ways. Observed from the outside, it might seem that they aren't necessarily protecting themselves or their children. This is where the naive question, "*Why doesn't she leave?*" comes into play. It is also where the more pervasive and dangerous belief of "*failure to protect*" is utilised by child protection services in particular.

The term failure to protect completely overlooks the resistance that a victim-survivor of domestic violence exerts, and it places the blame and responsibility for the violence wholly on the victim-survivor. The victim-survivor is judged not to be keeping the children safe. Rarely is the term failure to protect used to describe the perpetrator's actions. Thousands of children have been removed and placed into statutory care due to this mindset. Thousands of victim-survivors have been left unsupported and in danger.

The systems surrounding families and the general community have to profoundly change this entrenched belief system. Instead of considering the victim-survivor's actions as a failure to protect, imagine how different the conversation would be if we asked the question, *"How is the victim-survivor protecting their children despite the violence?"*

We have to change our values, beliefs and conversations to look at the victim-survivor's strengths. This is a fundamental aspect of the Safe and Together Framework. When I consider Emily's strengths, they are many and varied. The following list is just the tip of the iceberg:

- She chose and fought to become a teacher despite the violence.
- She chose to teach in the same school as her children so that she could ensure they had time with her throughout the day and on the way to and from school.
- She learnt to drive despite the control and abuse.
- She saved money from her salary to purchase a car.
- Her education provided her with knowledge about child development so she could meet her children's developmental needs, psychological, emotional and physical.
- She maintained her relationships with long-standing friends despite being physically isolated from them.
- She made new friends with people around her.
- She insisted her grandmother live with the family.

- She attempted to minimise the physical abuse and protect her children from trauma by complying with her husband's demands.

- She didn't leave because she knew she and her children would be in more danger.

- She didn't leave because she knew that if he were to fight her for custody, he would win, and her children would be prevented from having a relationship with her.

- She didn't leave because she was the protective parent and wanted to keep her children safe.

- She didn't leave because she knew that if she did, the violence would escalate.

- She didn't leave because she knew he would kill her if she did.

When we look at the situation through the eyes of the victim-survivor, we start to realise that everything they do is aimed at keeping themselves and their children alive. Everything a victim-survivor does to resist the violence, however troubling it may seem to the outside world, is to be lauded and seen as the most incredible strength.

What victim-survivors need from the community and system is support, not judgment. The question *"Why doesn't she leave?"* must also be understood within the entrenched failures of a system. The system supporting victim-survivors of domestic violence is grossly under-resourced and has been for decades. There are, quite simply, not enough beds. There are also restrictions surrounding safe placements. For example, it is almost impossible for mothers of teenage boys to find a place in a refuge.

Until very recently, financial abuse was not even considered. How is a victim-survivor supposed to leave when they have no access to bank accounts or money? How can a victim-survivor leave when they have nowhere to go? There is a significant affordable housing shortage in Australia and indeed, most of the world. Even if a victim-survivor could find somewhere to rent, how do they gather enough money for the bond and deposit? How do they get a loan when often they have no credit rating because the perpetrator has denied them access to a bank account?

It is even worse for migrant or refugee victim-survivors, who have often been denied the opportunity to learn English. They have been isolated from their cultural community specifically and from the wider community generally. They are caught in a trap of visa issues where they have been sponsored by the perpetrator, and if they leave the marriage, they will be deported, but their children will remain. Some migrant communities often, though significantly not always, do not perceive domestic violence for what it is because it is seen as the norm in their countries of origin.

Aboriginal women and children are appallingly over-represented in the ranks of victim-survivors of domestic violence. They face generational trauma, alcohol misuse, generational domestic violence, lack of employment, isolated communities, lack of adequate government support, lack of services, casual and direct racism and apathetic, judgemental and racist police officers and legal systems. The list of risk factors is seemingly endless for victim-survivors who are Aboriginal or Torres Strait Islander.

One of the most dangerous places for women, specifically when it comes to domestic violence, is within faith communities. In 2017, Julia Baird and Hayley Gleeson, two very well-respected journalists, conducted a year-long investigation into domestic violence within faith communities. If you do an internet search, there are a plethora of interviews and television programs discussing the results. They are deeply concerning.

In the eyes of the Western world, Muslim communities are often (wrongly) assumed and judged to have a terrible and entrenched issue with domestic violence. Domestic violence within a religious setting is pervasive across all faiths, and it is the Christian church that is one of the worst offenders. Sexist attitudes, naïveté about the prevalence of domestic violence and collusion with perpetrators are deeply held within Christian communities. Women are disbelieved and blamed daily. They are told it is their duty to adhere to their marriage vows. They are told to submit to their husbands. Young women are told not to wear anything vaguely revealing lest they lead men astray. I have never heard of a church leader asking men why they are lusting after young women who might happen to be wearing a sleeveless dress or a v-neck that comes down a little bit too far. Too many church leaders collude with perpetrators and gaslight women in the name of being a "good" Christian and following the bible. The perpetrator repeatedly tells victim-survivors that they won't be believed and will be cast out from their community, and that, in fact, is what happens.

According to the Australian War Memorial[20], 51 service personnel died during the Afghanistan and Iraq wars combined. In 2024, according to Destroy the Joint's Counting Dead Women project[21], 78 women in Australia were murdered. Apparently, it is more dangerous to be a woman in Australia than it is to be a member of the armed services in a war zone.

---

20 https://www.awm.gov.au/articles/encyclopedia/war_casualties
21 https://www.facebook.com/DestroyTheJoint?

Angharad Candlin

NINE

A few years after the accident that led to Emily's significant head injury, her husband decided to move the family closer to Hobart. He had successfully applied for a more senior role. Ellis was about to transition to high school, and it seemed to be the right time to move. Once again, Emily wasn't consulted. Once again, Emily was isolated from her now extensive support network.

Emily and her husband looked for a home and found a beautiful old house, which, once again, needed some work done. Emily was happy about the new project and loved the house. Worryingly though, once again, it was in a small community out of the main hub of Hobart and at least half an hour from any support services.

Out of the blue one evening, Emily called me. She was sobbing and barely coherent. I couldn't understand most of what she said, but in between her choking breaths, I heard, "*He keeps making me drink. He's forcing me to drink. I'm really scared. He beat me up*". I was completely confused and really worried. She sounded paranoid and in the depths of a mental health crisis. I almost asked her to put her husband on the phone so I could make some sense of what she was saying, but then she said, "*I'm at the back of the garden. He's coming, I have to go*". She abruptly hung up the phone. I tried to call back multiple times both that evening and in the ensuing days, weeks and months, but there was never any answer.

I couldn't drop everything and rush down to Tasmania. Life for me was chaotic and messy. I had just purchased a new house and recently moved in, was helping my sister plan her wedding to her fiancé who was yet to migrate to Australia, and dealing with our mum's Multiple Sclerosis relapse, whilst my father was temporarily overseas for work. Eventually, I tracked down a number for Emily's younger sister, Susannah, who was now living in Brisbane. I knew contacting Emily's father would have been fruitless.

I managed to piece together what had been happening in the years that Emily and my contact had been sporadic. Emily's husband had increasingly been using alcohol as a way to control her. Prior to every meal, when he was at home, he would insist Emily have a drink, such as a gin and tonic, and then during the meal, would force her to drink multiple glasses of wine. He insisted that he wanted a glass of wine but didn't want to drink alone, so Emily had to drink with him. What he did, however, was continually fill Emily's glass whilst he drank to excess. Emily protested, but he ignored her and forced her to drink even more. She was so scared of what he would do if she didn't comply, and in a desperate bid to protect her children from his violence, she felt she had no choice but to drink.

Whilst some might judge Emily for drinking too much, in reality, she was drinking to protect herself and her children. It was the only means she had to resist his violence.

There has been a significant amount of research in Australia and internationally about the intersection of drugs and alcohol and domestic violence. In Australia and most Western countries, the most violent periods of time are Christmas/New Year and sporting grand finals, particularly Rugby League and football/soccer.

According to Humphreys et al.[22] from Melbourne University, "*At least three decades of research on the intersection of substance use with domestic and family violence consistently shows the frequency, severity and impact of violence increases in the context of the perpetrator using alcohol and other drugs.*

Some 24–54% of domestic and family violence incidents reported to police in Australia are classified as alcohol-related, while other drugs are implicated in 1–9% of incidents. This is consistent with international evidence, which shows substance use occurs with domestic and family violence in 25–50% of cases.

Several studies have also pointed to the increased severity of domestic and family violence when substances are involved. An

---

22 The Conversation, 17th September 2024.

Australian study, which looked at 240 women murdered by a current or former male partner between 2010 and 2018, reports more than 60% of the male perpetrators were affected by alcohol or drugs during the fatal episode".

What has only recently become the subject of research is the use of drugs and alcohol in the control of victim-survivors. Emily's husband made a deliberate decision to turn his wife, who usually only drank alcohol on social occasions or a glass of wine at dinner at most, into an alcoholic.

Humphreys and colleagues[23] are particularly interested in the perpetrator's use of drugs and alcohol as a tool of coercive control:

"Perpetrators may also weaponise victim-survivors' substance use. Research shows that, to numb the physical and emotional pain of family violence, victim-survivors may start using substances.

Perpetrators often encourage this practice to increase their power and control over the victim-survivor and to undermine their credibility if authorities become involved.

Likewise, perpetrators may exacerbate victim-survivors' existing substance use, such as by pressuring them to drink or take drugs more often. Alternatively, they might sabotage victim-survivors' recovery efforts, preventing their access to treatment services.

Another tactic involves lying about the nature and extent of the victim-survivor's substance use. This can undermine their credibility with authorities such as child protection services or the family court."

Like me, Susannah had significant concerns about her brother-in-law and had observed the abusive way he spoke to and about Emily.

She also told me that when she had been visiting the family, Emily's husband, as usual, had been verbally abusive towards Emily. Susannah intervened and told him he needed to stop. Enraged that his sister-in-law would question him, he grabbed her by the hair, dragged her down the corridor from the lounge room to the kitchen, and then repeatedly punched and kicked her. All the time, Emily pleaded with him to stop, but he continued. Years later, when Emily described the incident in detail to me, she said he "*pulverised*" Susannah.

---

23 The Conversation, 17th September 2024.

The kitchen was right underneath the children's bedrooms and whilst they had been asleep, the screaming from Susannah and the noise from the violent assault had woken them. Emily's husband then went upstairs and ordered the children to come down and see their aunt, all the time telling them how pathetic she was as she lay on the floor rolled up in a ball, battered, bruised and bleeding. I cannot comprehend how terrified the children must have been. Emily managed to call the police during the assault. They quickly arrived, arrested him and held him overnight. Incredibly, they didn't apply for an AVO to protect Susannah, Emily or the children, and he was allowed to return home the following day.

Once he had been removed from the house, Emily rushed to pack bags for everyone, somehow managed to get tickets for the ferry to Melbourne and drove everyone back to Sydney to stay with her father. They didn't have time to get to the local Emergency Department. Emily was so petrified of what her husband would do once released. Her priority was to get everyone out of Tasmania immediately. Once in Sydney, she dropped the children off with her father and took Susannah to the local hospital. Susannah had severe bruising to her face, ribs, back, arms and legs, as well as some significant cuts that needed to be stitched and dressed. Miraculously, she didn't suffer any broken bones or internal injuries.

The children, Susannah and Emily, stayed with their father for about a month. Her husband utilised the court system to exert his power and control over Emily by reporting that she had kidnapped the children. As we know, Emily's husband could be charming and present himself very, very well. He portrayed Emily as a mentally unwell alcoholic and himself as a doting, protective father and man who loved his wife dearly and was committed to supporting his wife to recover. She was mandated to return to Tasmania with the children. In the meantime, the police compiled a brief of evidence for the Department of Public Prosecutions (DPP). The DPP decided that the matter should go to court.

Once she returned to Tasmania, Emily organised to see a therapist. The Principal of the school where she worked was very supportive of Emily. Whilst her husband made efforts to avoid leaving marks on parts of her body that were visible, there were times when his assaults were so severe that they left Emily with bruises to her face and arms. As Emily has said to me, *"There are only so many times you can tell your boss that you've fallen over or walked into a door"*. She had many supportive colleagues who were worried about her. One of them organised for Emily and the children to stay with her until the court case.

Emily engaged a lawyer to represent her. Her husband organised an expensive lawyer from a top law firm and a QC to represent him. He organised multiple character witnesses, including a neighbour who had once seen Emily alcohol-affected. Numerous friends and colleagues of Emily made themselves available as character witnesses for her. Emily's therapist told her that the domestic violence she was experiencing was the worst she had ever seen. She requested to give evidence.

The husband's legal team objected to each of her character witnesses and to the therapist. The Judge upheld the objection. Emily's husband went into court armed with multiple character witnesses. She was allowed none. The case that the husband made was that Emily was still suffering the ill effects of her head injury, was an alcoholic, an un-protective parent and psychiatrically unwell.

Emily's sister was persuaded by her father that she shouldn't give evidence as it would be too distressing. Without Susannah's evidence, the only voice heard in court was that of the husband and the police evidence. Emily's evidence was dismissed as hearsay.

The Judge had reservations about both parents, so he made orders that the children be removed and placed with the paternal grandmother. He made orders for Emily to attend a residential psychiatric unit for treatment. No orders or consequences were put in place for the perpetrator.

Once the Judge and lawyers withdrew, Emily was gathering her things, and as she looked up she realised she was alone in the courtroom with her husband across the room. He smiled and blew kisses to her. She was repulsed. When he exited the courtroom, he was drawn into the circle of his family. He collapsed sobbing on the floor in front of them whilst they comforted him. He was a master of manipulation, even with his own family. Emily told me this detail when we were discussing this book. I wanted to vomit with disgust when I heard what he had done.

Emily was distraught at the thought of being separated from her children. She insisted that there was nothing wrong with her, that she didn't have a psychiatric condition and that she was the victim of domestic violence. The response from the psychiatric hospital was that she could either stay for a week or two voluntarily or she would be held against her will on a "psychiatric hold" for three months. Unsurprisingly, Emily chose to stay for the week voluntarily.

With that decision, her fate was sealed. She had made an admission that she was psychiatrically unwell, and her husband had evidence that she did indeed have a psychiatric condition. A "fact" that he could now use at his whim to negate anything she said in defence of herself and in accusations about her perpetrator.

Hearing how the legal system failed Emily and her children enraged me beyond belief. I cannot count the number of times I have heard similar stories as part of my work, but this was personal. This was my best friend. This is the reality of the court system. It doesn't seem to matter what country is involved; in Australia, the USA, the UK, and Canada, the court system is just another abusive system for victim-survivors.

The court case happened just before Christmas. For the first time in her life, Emily was separated from her children over what should have been the festive season. I don't recall how I discovered where Emily was, but I rang her on Christmas Day. She was desolate and inconsolable.

The perpetrator decided that his mother should care for the children in the family home. She moved in, but of course, contrary to the legal orders, he also stayed at home. Effectively, he remained with the children while Emily was completely separated from them.

Once she was discharged, she went to stay with one of her most supportive friends and colleagues. She remained with her for several months. She was only allowed to see the children, under the supervision of child protective services, about once a week. Eventually, following the required three-month supervision order, Emily was allowed to move back home. One could question why Emily, having escaped the abuse, chose to move back home. Her answer is clear: "*To protect the children*". Having had this experience in the court system, she knew that if she were to ever leave, she would not be awarded custody of the children. The perpetrator would once again use the legal system to ensure her parental responsibility was severed and awarded solely to him, and she would never have any access to her children.

Now, looking back on this event over twenty years later, Emily is certain that if her sister had given evidence, her current reality would have looked very different from what it is now.

When we think about coercive control, it is essential that we see the abuse as a pattern of behaviour, not as a single incident. The Safe and Together's[24] framework is clear; if we are to address domestic violence effectively, we must look at it through a broader lens than the traditional incident-based approach. A much more effective way of viewing and understanding domestic violence is using a Perpetrator Pattern and a Multiple Pathways to Harm approach.

Importantly, using the Safe and Together framework means we look through the lens of perpetrator and victim-survivor rather than gender. We think about the non-offending parent and the offending parent. We think about the perpetrator's pattern of behaviour as a parenting choice.

The Multiple Pathways to Harm framework examines "*...the perpetrator's pattern of behaviour and the resulting harm or risk of harm to children through multiple pathways including:*

1. *The emotional and physical safety of the child.*

2. *The effect of the partner's parenting.*

3. *The effect on the family ecology.*"

Furthermore, if we use a perpetrator pattern approach rather than an incident-based approach, we get a much better picture of what is happening. The critical components to consider are:

- *The perpetrator's pattern of coercive control.*
- *The actions taken by the perpetrator to harm the child.*

---

24 https://safeandtogetherinstitute.com

- *The full spectrum of the non-offending parent's efforts to promote the safety and wellbeing of the child.*

- *The adverse impact of the perpetrator's behaviour on the child.*

- *The role of substance abuse, mental health, culture and other sociology-economic factors.*

The third significant factor to consider is intersections and intersectionalities. Intersections refer to the point where domestic violence intersects with an individual's other significant issues, such as drug and alcohol use, mental and physical ill health, disability and so on. Intersectionalities refer to wider social structures that can influence the context of domestic violence, such as gender, culture, religion and sexuality, for example.

The questions to ask are:

- What is the perpetrator doing to *cause* mental health or substance abuse issues?

- What is the perpetrator doing to *exacerbate* problems that already exist?

- What is the perpetrator doing to *interfere* with the support and treatment that the victim needs?

Looking at the abuse perpetrated against Emily, it is clear that her husband used alcohol as a pattern of coercive control. He caused Emily's substance abuse issues.

Considering the assault on Susannah when the children were upstairs in bed and when he subsequently brought them downstairs to see her cowering on the floor, it is clear that his behaviour was adversely impacting his children and their emotional safety was significantly compromised. He chose to be violent. He chose to ensure his children experienced it. He used violence as a parenting choice. This was, without a doubt, child abuse.

For too long, the prevailing opinion has been that unless perpetrators directly assault, abuse, or neglect their children, the children have not been harmed. When we look at what happened with Emily's children, it is clear that they were harmed by their father's pattern of behaviour towards his wife, including the single incident where he assaulted his sister-in-law. Victim-survivors of domestic violence include the adults and the children equally. The children must be treated with the same care as the adult victim-survivor.

Angharad Candlin

TEN

Following the ordeal of the court case and once things had returned to some semblance of normality, Emily knew she needed help to treat her alcohol addiction. She was referred to a residential treatment program for 12 weeks. It was agony being separated from her children, but Emily committed to the program. During her time there, she was supported to complete some Life Story work, including a timeline of major events in her life and of the abuse. Here, she was safe to process the complexity of her life and the relentless abuse at the hands of her husband. She knew for the sake of her children that she couldn't leave her marriage, but she committed herself to being sober.

Her husband picked her up from the centre when she was discharged and instead of returning home, took her to the pub. Emily was horrified. I was horrified when she told me. She was too scared of him to object. He asked her what she wanted to drink. She asked for tonic water. He ordered her a gin and tonic. This was a man who was supposed to love and cherish her. He had made vows to honour her. Instead, he destroyed her.

This one experience reveals the nuances of coercive control. Going back to the man on the Clapham omnibus theory from Chapter 2, there is nothing inherently wrong with a husband taking his wife out for a drink at the pub. On its own, no reasonable person would think anything of it. Viewed in context, however, nobody could say that this behaviour was remotely acceptable.

Despite the coercive control and in the face of never-ending assaults, rapes, shaming and gaslighting, Emily remained sober for another ten years. I am incredibly proud of her.

Emily lived for the times when he was away with work. She could spend time being the mother she wanted to be to her children without interference. She could also focus on her work. She successfully applied for the role of Deputy Principal at a School for Specific Purposes (SSP). A K-12 school specifically targeted to children who had disengaged from the education system.

She loved this job. She loved supporting her colleagues, forming relationships with the children and seeing them blossom within the school environment. She was highly respected at work and within their small community. She was remunerated well in this job and was in a position where she was being paid more than her husband. He hated this.

When he was at home, he took every opportunity to degrade Emily. He regularly called her a disgrace and an embarrassment. He continued to question her competence as a result of the head injury. Whenever Emily queried her husband, whenever she did something he didn't approve of, whenever she refused to do something, he would assault her in the most severe and horrific ways.

I visited Emily during this time. She met me at the airport, and we went to High Tea together as a treat. We had a wonderful couple of hours catching up together, just the two of us. She seemed really well, loved her job and told me all about it. She filled me in on the children, their exploits and plans for their futures. I asked her how things were with her husband. She told me things were not good but that they had both *"behaved badly"* and were working on it in counselling.

I stayed for the weekend with Emily and spent time with the children, all in their late adolescence/early adulthood by now. It was great to see them. We went out for dinner together that evening without their father, who was apparently working. Nothing seemed amiss. There was no sign of the torment she was experiencing, nor what the children had endured for their entire lives. Emily's husband avoided me, and I only saw him very briefly when he took Patrick off for a camping trip the following day.

Emily enjoyed the work in her new school, and the school clearly valued her input. The school became involved in a project where schools from around Australia and the Pacific basin participated in exchange programs to learn from each other. Emily was nominated to represent her school. It was a year-long project, and she would be away for a few days at a time once a month. Her husband was livid. As usual, he did everything he could to undermine her. She was determined to participate, regardless of his fury and accompanying behaviour.

Eventually, it came time for her school to host the delegation. On the final evening, Emily organised a social gathering at her house. They had a lovely garden, it was Spring, and the weather was good. The guests arrived. But in his precise and menacing way, her husband barred her from going downstairs to meet everyone. He threatened to make a scene if she dared show her face.

Emily remained upstairs until her husband relented about an hour into the event and allowed her to go downstairs. She was embarrassed; her Principal had been forced to "host" the event whilst Emily's husband fabricated reasons for her absence. Emily had no idea what he said to the guests, but it was clear that he created a situation that made her look unreliable in front of her colleagues. Once again, his choice of coercive control was chipping away at Emily's reputation and her sense of self.

During this period, Emily and her husband were advised by their GP to attend relationship counselling. Initially, the counselling utilised a "shuttle" or "relay" framework. This is where the parties are in separate rooms, and the counsellor moves between them. Eventually, the counselling moved into a more traditional couple therapy framework. Emily and her husband were in a room together with the therapist.

Emily found herself being railroaded by both her husband and the counsellor time after time. He, of course, as usual, presented as the rational party, painting a picture of Emily's dysfunction. Emily would find herself repeatedly saying, "*No, that's not right, that's not what happened*". He would strongly assert that it was. Emily would be overwhelmed and frustrated by this and would often end up in tears. She recalls that on one occasion, she refused to back down in opposition to the picture that was being painted. The discussion became heated and aggressive; in response, the counsellor ran out of the room in tears, and her supervisor took over the session.

When inexperienced or ill-trained relationship counsellors provide "relationship counselling" in situations that are actually domestic violence, the violence is mislabelled as "conflict" or even "high conflict". When domestic violence is misconstrued as conflict, the assumption is made that the conflict is mutual. Each party has equal power, and both are equally inflicting harm. As I mentioned earlier, this may also be referred to as "mutualised" violence or as "situational couple violence".

Effective relationship counselling relies on both parties truly having equal power. Referring couples to relationship counselling when one party is perpetrating violence is completely unacceptable and, in fact, dangerous. The profound risk is that counsellors who have not participated in specialist domestic violence training, particularly around the nuances of coercive control, will be groomed by the perpetrator. The counsellor is then at risk of colluding with the perpetrator against the victim-survivor.

This does a great injustice to the victim-survivor in a multitude of ways; essentially, their story, if they even have an opportunity to articulate it, is disbelieved, the perpetrator's account of the relationship becomes "the truth", and victim-survivors don't receive the support they desperately need. Not only that, but the perpetrator uses whatever the victim-survivor might have said in the room to inflict more violence. It also reinforces the perpetrator's position as the rational, well-functioning party, and they can then use this apparent validation from the "expert" counsellor to perpetrate even more abuse.

Where there is a past history or current experience of domestic violence, or even in cases where the counsellor suspects violence of any kind is being perpetrated, the parties must be seen individually.

All relationship counsellors have a duty to their clients to participate in intensive, appropriate and evidence-based domestic violence training prior to commencing any work with couples. As I have indicated throughout this book, my preferred framework is Safe and Together, which has been rolled out worldwide. Further, they must have a process for adequate intake and assessment of couples and to screen each member of the couple individually, as a matter of course, for domestic violence.

My advice to individuals seeking counselling where domestic violence is present is to research the counsellor thoroughly. Ask the counsellor if they have attended specialist domestic violence training. Ask them which training they attended and how long it was. Ask them if they receive regular clinical supervision. If the answer to any of these questions is no, I would encourage that person to find another counsellor. If the answer to the specialist training is something like half or one day, then I would advise finding a different counsellor.

Screening for domestic violence is improving. Most government and large non-government agencies routinely screen for domestic violence. In the private counselling sector, however, unfortunately, DV screening is patchy at best. It is also essential that relationship counsellors have regular clinical supervision by an experienced supervisor. Again, in my experience as a retired Board Authorised Clinical Supervisor for many years, this, too, is often woefully inadequate in the private sector.

Many times, Emily's husband beat her so severely that she would end up, just as her sister had done, cowering on the floor a bruised and terrified wreck. Once he was done with her, he would go upstairs, wake the children, and make them come down to observe their mother shaking on the floor. All the time telling them what a pathetic, alcoholic woman and mother she was. He presented to his children as a strong, caring, loving parent, and he led them to believe that it was entirely Emily's fault that she was curled up on the floor. He told them it was her alcoholism that caused her to be so *"pathetic"* despite the fact that she was entirely sober. He was very careful when he assaulted her to leave no cuts or bruises on visible parts of her body. Emotional abuse can be even more damaging and certainly longer lasting than physical abuse.

When considering the impact of domestic violence on children, I hope readers will be able to see the clear connection between witnessing domestic violence and child abuse. It is not just directly observing or experiencing the violence that is abusive. Seeing and experiencing the effects and impact of the abuse on the protective parent is equally damaging. Further, when children are living in a violent environment, they are in a constant state of threat. When a person experiences a stressful experience, the cortisol and adrenaline within their bodies flood the brain. When brains are inundated with these neurochemicals, they stop growing and developing as they should. Individuals move into a state of fight, flight or freeze.

Imagine children living in a violent environment where one parent is being terrorised by the other parent. Their brains are constantly in a state of hyper-arousal in fight, flight or freeze mode. They can't learn anything new, they don't get good sleep, they can't focus, they can't relax, they can't maintain friendships, they may self-harm, and they may attempt or complete suicide. The impact of chronic stress on children's brains is profound. There is a plethora of research regarding the long-term damage caused to children by domestic violence. Domestic violence is child abuse, irrespective of whether the children directly experience it or not.

Equally worrying is the impact of a mother's chronic stress on a developing foetus. The neurochemicals that flood the mother's system when domestic violence is present transfer into the developing child. This causes what is known as epigenetic changes in the brains of the infant. This means that unborn infants experience the violence, and they are born sensitised to chronic stress. Quite literally, domestic violence changes the brain's architecture in the developing foetus. Emily's husband not only abused her, he abused his children.

In 2017, Howard-Belle[25] described the results of in-depth interviews she conducted with 17 Australian male perpetrators of domestic violence involved in Men's Behaviour Change Programs. The participants disclosed a number of ways they purposely chose to destroy the mother-child bond. *"The majority of men described using such tactics in order to derail maternal power and authority. They were aware of the deleterious impact that these tactics had on the ability of their partners to enjoy being a mother and to parent their children effectively. However, no man expressed concern or remorse about the impact on women and children."*

Further:

"A number of mothers were described as suffering from alcohol and substance abuse problems, which men believed limited their ability to adequately mother their children. Quite apart from their

---

25 Exploiting the 'good mother' as a tactic of coercive control: Domestically violent men's assaults on women as mothers, Journal of Women and Social Work Vol 32(3), pp374-389

accounts of the potential emotional and/or psychological impact of domestic violence on their partners, 8 men constructed partners and ex-partners as women with a multitude of mental health and/or drug and alcohol problems. They did not perceive of these "problems" as being related to the abusive and oppressive circumstances that they had directly created through their use of violence and other coercively controlling behaviours. In their view, women had pre-existing conditions.

"Many men described actively teaching their children to disrespect and abuse their mothers."

The tactics that Emily's husband employed are typical behaviours of men who perpetrate domestic violence. It is almost as though there is a guidebook for perpetrators. As far as I am aware, there isn't. These are not men who "*snapped*". These are not men who "*were driven to it*". The almost unbelievable similarity in the behaviours reveals the pervasive nature of domestic violence. If these perpetrators had acted out of an acute and abnormal time of stress, the behaviours wouldn't be identical across all communities, all socio-economic, all cultural, and all religious groups.

The choice to consistently degrade Emily in front of her children over decades has had a terrible and ongoing impact in many ways.

I visited Emily last year, a couple of months after her daughter gave birth to twins. Emily's first grandchildren: a boy and a girl. She had sent me photos of them and was incredibly excited about their arrival. She was doing well in terms of her alcohol misuse and was looking forward to seeing them. Not long before I arrived, Hannah told her mother that she couldn't see the babies because she couldn't trust her not to harm them.

Emily would never harm anyone. She is the most kind and gentle person I know, even when she has been using alcohol. I have been friends with Emily for what seems like forever. I am the person who arguably knows her the best, and I'm definitely her closest friend. I contacted Hannah, appealing for her to let Emily see her first grandchildren. I reassured her that I would be there. As a community psychologist, I have supported dozens of vulnerable mums when they have seen their children. I am exceptionally well qualified to ensure the babies would be safe; after all, Hannah and her husband would also be there.

Hannah was adamant that she would not allow Emily to see her children until she was *"well and truly sober"*. I could hear the echo of her husband's voice in the words that Hannah used. I could hear the decades of deliberate alienation of the children from Emily. I could hear his systematic interference in Emily's mother-child bond with her daughter. I could hear the disrespect and abuse of Emily by her daughter in that simple word *"no"*.

What this simple word did was to send Emily spiralling down into using alcohol once again, despite being an active participant in a community drug and alcohol service and having been sober for a number of months. It was like a sharp slap in her face. This is yet another example of the coercive control her husband had perpetrated and now passed on to the next generation. As a result of his deliberate choice to annihilate Emily, he can continue to abuse her from a distance. I doubt that anyone looking at this situation on the surface would comprehend that this is the continuing pattern of his coercive control.

Alcoholism is a disease. In Emily's case, it is a disease purposely inflicted by her husband. She has protected her children from the knowledge of the depths of the abuse she experienced at the hands of their father. She is gracious and loving of Hannah and far more forgiving than I am. She thinks it will distress her children considerably if they are truly aware of their father's depravity. She's probably right, but as her friend, I feel it is deeply unfair, and I have been, and continue to be, tempted to tell them just how awful their father is. However, I respect Emily's wishes - the last thing she needs or deserves is for her best friend to betray her trust.

The children are now all adults with fully independent lives. For decades, the messages that Emily's husband has asserted and continues to assert are that Emily is dangerous, she is abusive, she is an alcoholic, and she is psychiatrically unwell. She can't be trusted. He has held fast to that promise that he first made in the early days of their relationship; *"If we ever part, I will destroy you... "*. He may not have murdered her, but he certainly destroyed her. She is a shell of the woman I once knew.

Her children are just as much the victims of his coercive control as Emily. It is devastating.

Angharad Candlin

ELEVEN

Mutualising domestic violence - framing it or dismissing it as a conflict between a married couple - is a common occurrence. It is commonly viewed this way by wider society and often by the systems surrounding families. Domestic violence is not conflict. Domestic violence is coercive control. It is financial control. It is religious and cultural control, it is sexual and physical assault, it is stalking, it is gaslighting, it is murder. It is not an argument between two equal parties.

Considering the perpetrator's pattern of behaviour provides us with a clearer picture of who the primary aggressor is, particularly when we take into account ways the victim-survivor may resist the violence. For the sake of easier reading, I will use gendered language in the following example. A male partner has a history of perpetrating violence upon the female partner. He approaches his partner in the kitchen in an extremely aggressive manner, shouting that he will kill her as he reaches to put his hands around her throat. In desperation, the female partner grabs the knife she has been using to cut up the vegetables for dinner and manages to slash his arm. Neighbours have heard the commotion and called the police. The police arrive within minutes and knock on the door. The male, now covered in blood, answers the door and tells the police that his partner has "*gone crazy*" and, for no reason, has slashed him with a knife. He tells them that his wife has been receiving treatment for Bipolar disorder.

In the midst of a chaotic situation like the one described above, police will generally arrest the female partner because she has the knife and she inflicted an injury. If, however, police speak to each individual involved alone, with a pattern-based approach, it is much easier for them to see that the male partner has a pattern of aggressive and abusive behaviour and has, in fact, harmed his wife on multiple occasions but she has been too afraid to seek assistance. The husband is the primary aggressor, not the wife.

A second problem that arises when domestic violence is referred to as conflict is exactly what Emily described to me. She told me on multiple occasions that she was equally responsible for the conflict and that they had *"both behaved badly"*. They were referred for and had commenced relationship counselling. The perpetrator of the violence should rather be referred to a specialist domestic violence program for assessment, whilst the victim-survivor is referred, for example, to trauma-based counselling. Remembering, of course, that children are also victim-survivors and should receive age-appropriate counselling and support.

A couple of years after my visit, Jen, Emily's close friend and flatmate from university, visited them for the weekend. She regularly visited the family and had a close relationship with the children. Over the years, she observed the derogatory comments and controlling behaviour that Emily had endured. Like me, she was concerned for Emily and the children's wellbeing. I had met Jen a couple of times when Emily was at university. She struck me as being strong, confident, vivacious and funny. Following university, she forged a successful career for herself and had a son within a long-term relationship, which unfortunately ended when her son was relatively young. I always thought Jen was the kind of person who wouldn't stand for nonsense from anyone. I was glad Emily had such a long-standing and close friendship.

Emily had been increasingly confident that her husband was having an affair. She felt that it would be safest to broach the matter with him whilst Jen was there, certain that he would not assault her in Jen's presence.

It was Saturday evening after the children were in bed. Emily and Jen had spent a couple of hours curled up on the lounge talking about life in general, as good friends who haven't seen each other in a while do. Jen dozed off, and Emily went into the kitchen to finish cleaning up after dinner. Her husband was in the kitchen and had done the majority of the work. Emily thought this would be a good time to raise the issue of his affair.

I have never heard Emily shout at anyone nor speak badly of anyone. I have no doubt that she approached this topic with care and trepidation, given the decades of abuse she had endured. She wanted to know if her suspicions were accurate. The niggling feelings about the vague explanations of her husband's whereabouts and his frequent absences had been going on for years.

Emily quietly asked him if he was seeing someone else. As she finished her sentence, she saw a look of fury on his face that she hadn't seen before. He almost spat the words at her that she was being paranoid, that she was the one who had spent her life flirting with men, that she was the one who embarrassed him with her behaviour, that she was the one who had multiple affairs. Then he said words Emily never thought he would say; *"If you think I've been having sex with other women, I might as well fuck Jen and you're going to watch"*.

He didn't care that his children were in bed asleep upstairs. He was intent on raping Jen. Unable to find a condom, he paused to grab a small freezer bag to use instead. He pulled Emily by her hair into the living room, where Jen was still sleeping on the sofa. Emily was distraught as she watched her husband grab her friend, hold her down with one hand and rip her clothes off with the other. He demanded that Emily watch as he violently raped Jen. Emily and Jen both screamed, totally terrified of this monster. Emily couldn't watch this frenzied assault on her friend. She turned her back and tried to get away, desperate because although she tried to pull him off, she couldn't do anything to stop it.

This was the most horrific act of violence that he perpetrated. Both women feared for their lives. Neither were in a position to call the police. They were too terrified to move or even speak. After the rape, he left the two women shaking and sobbing, totally traumatised and went to bed. The next day, he acted as if nothing had happened.

I understand why Emily felt that she couldn't call the police. Their manifestly inadequate response to the assault on her sister years before, the lack of AVO, only spending one night in detention, the nightmare court case. If it went to court this time, given his access to money and high profile Barristers, along with her history of alcohol abuse, she knew she would have no chance. It would actually make things even more dangerous for her because he would be so infuriated.

When I interviewed Emily for this book, knowing how strong and confident Jen was, I asked why Jen didn't report the rape. Emily told me that Jen, too, was terrified of Emily's abuser and didn't think she would be believed. She was also afraid Emily would ostracise her, and she would lose her relationship with Emily and the children. Emily has never recovered from this incident. She is still traumatised by it. She has talked to me about it a number of times over the ensuing years, and each time, I can see her visibly shake with fear and distress.

The police response to matters of domestic violence has long been an issue of great concern. There is very little evidence-based information about police responses to domestic violence in the early 1990s to late 2000s. Anecdotally, there are many stories of police failures over decades, across all of the states, and indeed, broadly speaking, the world, when it comes to their response to domestic violence. Not only do the police find it difficult to assess the primary aggressor, they regularly minimise domestic violence. Despite receiving training, they are still ill-equipped to respond to domestic violence. There is also a small but significant proportion of police officers who are perpetrators of domestic violence themselves and rely on each other to conceal their actions and to harass, intimidate or stalk their victims.

Whilst all states have different laws, generally speaking, the response of the police is pretty similar irrespective of which state or even which Western country. There are, however, some helpful measures to compare police responses over time in NSW.

In 2006, the NSW Ombudsman[26] released a special report to Parliament. The views of service providers were sought. In summary, particular concerns related to:

- *Delays by police in responding to incidents.*
- *Failure to act on reported breaches of ADVOs.*

---

26 https://www.ombo.nsw.gov.au/reports/report-to-parliament/domestic-violence-improving-police-practice-special-report-to-parliament-december-2006

- *Failure to fully investigate domestic violence incidents.*
- *Inadequate support and follow-up.*

Other major findings related to:

- *No comprehensive framework to plan for domestic violence responses.*
- *No tools for frontline police.*
- *No standardised risk assessment.*
- *Out-of-date procedures to guide police.*
- *No investigation kits.*
- *Lack of quality and quantity of training.*

In 2023, the Law Enforcement Conduct Commission[27] released its report into the Review of NSW Police Force responses to domestic and family violence. The review focussed on complaints made between 1st July 2017 and the 1st July 2021. The complaints fell into two categories:

- *Officers being involved in domestic and family violence incidents:*

  70 out of 222 complaint investigations comprised 60 police officers being involved in domestic and family violence incidents. Seventeen of the officers were charged. Eleven had been previously investigated.

- Inadequate investigations into reported domestic and family violence incidents.

The most concerning issues were:

- ○ *Failure to make a record of the reported incident.*
- ○ *Victim statements not taken or incomplete.*
- ○ *No witness statements were sought.*
- ○ *Inadequate supervision of the investigation.*

---

27 https://www.lecc.nsw.gov.au/news-and-publications/publications/review-of-nsw-police-force-responses-to-family-and-domestic-violence-incidents.pdf/@@download/file

    ○   *No victim support was provided.*

    ○   *Failure to collect suitable evidence.*

    ○   *Police did not apply for an ADVO (Apprehended Domestic Violence Order).*

In the almost 20 years between these reports, it seems that little has changed or improved. I am appalled that the very people who are supposed to be upholding the law are perpetrating the same crimes that they are investigating.

Again, responding to the inevitable question of *'Why doesn't she leave?'*, we only need to look at the considerable issues with police structure and responses to answer that question, coupled with a poor court process and outcomes. Women feel safer to stay, where they can predict the behaviour of an abuser than to leave. According to Australia's National Research Organisation for Women's Safety (ANROWS)[28] *"Women are most at risk of being killed or seriously harmed during and/or immediately after separation"*.

On the question of why Emily or Jen didn't report the rape - there are similar failures of police when it comes to believing and supporting victim-survivors of rape. It is not just the police who are responsible for the outcomes in situations of domestic violence. The court system is fraught with decisions that make the lives of women and children more dangerous.

As I mentioned earlier, in NSW, on 1st July 2024, coercive control became a criminal offence in and of itself. Many jurisdictions across the Western world and the different states within Australia have already brought or are bringing legislation responding to coercive control into law.

As I mentioned earlier, the first perpetrator was charged under the new laws less than a month after the legislation was passed. He was found guilty and sentenced on the 10th December 2024. The ABC successfully applied to access the court transcripts. Their report on the 10th December explains[29]:

---

28 https://www.anrows.org.au/publication/national-risk-assessment-principles-for-domestic-and-family-violence/read/ Appendix 1

29 https://www.abc.net.au/news/2024-12-10/first-coercive-control-nsw-sentencing/104706470?utm_source=abc_news_app&utm_medium=content_shared&utm_campaign=abc_news_app&utm_content=safari

"The man was also sentenced for other domestic violence offences, including assault occasioning actual bodily harm and stalking/intimidation intending fear of physical harm.

The NSW Police prosecution told Magistrate Pauline Wright the man perpetrated the acts in a home where children were present and the doors were locked. "She was locked inside ... the doors were shut with a padlock used," she said. The prosecution said the man told the woman: "This will be your last night, I am going to murder you".

Magistrate Wright heard the man controlled the woman's finances and access to her phone and moved her away from her support network, where the abuse intensified. The man had pleaded guilty to the charges but told the court on Tuesday that he was not a violent man.

NSW Police urged Magistrate Wright to consider the victim's safety.

"[The offender has] no indication of any remorse," the prosecutor said.

"[We are] asking you to consider the safety of the complainant as paramount." Magistrate Wright told the court the "facts are disturbing" and sentenced him to an 18-month intensive corrections order to be served in the community. The prosecution requested an electronic ankle monitor be issued, which the magistrate agreed to. The man was also instructed to participate in 120 hours of community service.

The outcome of this charge is, in my opinion, wholly inadequate. When perpetrators of violence are allowed to walk freely in the community and are not incarcerated for a period of time, victim-survivors - both adults and children - remain in grave danger.

According to the NSW Bureau of Crime Statistics and Research (BOCSAR)[30], in 2023/2024, 20% of domestic violence-related AVOs were breached. It is difficult to find an accurate figure for the number of parole breaches in relation to domestic violence offences.

---

30 https://bocsar.nsw.gov.au/topic-areas/domestic-violence.html

Angharad Candlin

TWELVE

It is difficult to digest the realities of living with domestic violence. Whilst I would like to say Emily's experience is unusual, sadly, it isn't. The statistics are sobering.

In NSW, according to BOCSAR[31]:

- *1 in 4 women and 1 in 8 men have experienced violence by an intimate partner or family member since the age of 18.*

- *In 2024, there were 38,272 reported cases of DV assault.*

- *In 2024, in NSW alone, there were 39 domestic violence-related murders: 13 adult men, 16 adult women and 10 children. The incidents included current and former intimate partners, family members, other household members, carers and ex-partner of current partner.*

- *28 offenders were male, and six were female*

- *In the 5 years to the end of 2024, in 40% of intimate partner murders, the offender was a current partner, and in 44% the offender was a current or ex-boyfriend/girlfriend.[32]I*

After the horrific incident with Jen, the abuse continued. It was relentless. Eventually, Emily's abuser ground her down so far that she found it impossible to resist the alcohol that he was still attempting to control her with. It was just too difficult. After months of drinking,

---

31 https://bocsar.nsw.gov.au/documents/topic-areas/domestic-violence/ Domestic_Violence_Quarterly_Trends_Report.pdf

32 https://bocsar.nsw.gov.au/documents/topic-areas/murder/DV_Murder_ Infographic.pdf

Emily summoned remarkable strength to seek out a second drug and alcohol treatment centre during the long school holidays. This time, it was for women only, and it was in Melbourne. She booked herself in. The program had several stages over a number of months that residents needed to complete prior to discharge.

We know that domestic violence is pervasive and widespread. If we are to support victim-survivors and indeed work with perpetrators, we must consider, until proven otherwise, that the primary issue (in this case, alcohol abuse) may be intersecting with domestic violence. Emily was asked once by a male counsellor whether there had been domestic violence, and Emily affirmed that there had been. His response was to ask her how she "*provoked*" her abuser. At the end of the conversation, he told Emily he thought the root of her problems was that she was "*fundamentally lazy*".

Despite this experience, Emily liked being with women, and in this treatment centre, she felt safe and supported. For the whole time Emily was in the centre, this man was assigned as her counsellor. Is it any wonder that Emily didn't speak more about the violence she had received over decades? This may have been the best opportunity for someone to discover the depth of the abuse she had experienced; instead, she was judged harshly. I spent much of the time that I interviewed Emily trying to control my feelings. This time, my anger as a former psychologist and board-authorised supervisor was barely controllable. How dare a professional who should know better treat his clients like this?

Her alcohol addiction was treated, and she had time and space for her mental health to recover from the trauma she had experienced. But nobody was curious as to why she had started drinking again, and after the mandated period, she was discharged - straight back to the abusive situation she had left. As a testament to her incredible resilience, she didn't relapse once she went home and remained sober for years.

In Chapter 9, I mention the concept of intersections and intersectionalities. On numerous occasions, the domestic violence Emily was experiencing intersected with psychiatric support and drug & alcohol treatment centres. Emily's abuser insisted on multiple occasions over the years that she be assessed by a psychiatrist. Each assessment has confirmed that Emily has never had any kind of psychiatric illness. Despite these assessments, her abuser was able to use the very fact that Emily had been assessed in his false narrative that she was mentally unwell, something he continues to do.

When systems only focus on their specialist area, they can become tunnel-visioned and miss all of the other warning signs of the co-occurrence of multiple issues. In the community services sector, it is commonplace to hear the term "dual diagnosis", which refers to the co-occurrence of drug/alcohol addiction and mental health. What we do not generally hear about is Intersection, particularly when it relates to domestic violence.

There is an even more significant issue when it comes to the intersection between drug & alcohol addiction and domestic violence. One of the core tenets of recovery is that the addict contacts family, friends and others to take responsibility and apologise for their behaviour. I asked Emily about her attendance at AA. She told me she couldn't bring herself to go because of the pressure put on her to make amends and apologise to her family, including her abuser. This dogmatic principle is actually getting in the way of the support and healing Emily needs.

When we consider addiction within the context of coercive control, addiction fellowships, such as AA, increase the risk to the victim-survivor and expect them to take responsibility, once again, for the behaviour of the perpetrator. This is unacceptable, and fellowship groups must take this into account when working with victim-survivors of domestic violence.

So often, our default position is to judge a person's motives and behaviour based on our own experiences of the world. None of us know what we would do if we found ourselves in Emily's situation. What we all need to do is to be curious. What was it that caused Emily to become addicted to alcohol? Was it loss and grief over the premature death of her mother? Was it a response to a distant father? Was it a history of horrific abuse at the hands of her husband? If we don't ask the curious questions, we miss the truth, and we lose the opportunity to help.

Even if we do ask curious, non-judgmental questions, there is no guarantee that a victim-survivor will disclose. If they don't, it's often that they don't feel safe. Or they fear they won't be believed. Or they fear a child protection report will be made. Or they fear that the police will be called, which will make things even more dangerous. Or they fear that the person they tell will collude with the perpetrator. Or they fear that they will be told they have to keep their marriage vows. The reasons are infinite. We need to be led by the victim-survivor. To not advise them but truly partner with them. To know without a shadow of a doubt that they are the expert in knowing the perpetrator and what they will do. To know that everything a victim-survivor does is to keep themselves and their children alive. Even if we don't understand it.

I knew things were bad within Emily's family. I asked her repeatedly over the years how she was. She trusted me implicitly. She knew I believed her about the abuse, and yet she still couldn't bring herself to tell me how terrible it was. I should have done better. If it happens again with another friend, I will do better.

In late November 2013, Emily felt a small lump at the side of her breast, almost under her armpit. She wasn't concerned but nevertheless made an appointment with her GP. Her GP, realising this could potentially be very serious, organised an immediate emergency consultation with breast cancer specialists in Hobart. Emily had no time to process what was happening. Her husband came with her for this first appointment. He grumbled about having to take time off work for what he was sure would turn out to be nothing. He stayed in the waiting room.

Emily had an ultrasound, which showed a suspicious mass. Then, she had a needle biopsy and blood tests. She had to remove her clothes, her breasts exposed as various medical specialists examined her. She felt completely alone and vulnerable. The various tests came back positive for Triple Negative breast cancer. The specialists discussed her options with her. Due to the aggressive nature of the cancer, she decided to have a double mastectomy rather than a lumpectomy. The specialists decided that given the severity of the diagnosis, Emily would best be served by having treatment at the Royal Women and Children's Hospital in Melbourne.

Emily reflected that it was whilst she was being diagnosed with cancer that she had space to think about herself. Just herself. Not appeasing her husband, not caring for her children, not worrying about her job. She spent time considering the impact of treatment on how she would look and how she would feel. She knew she would look different, and she knew she would lose her beautiful, long, dark hair. She contemplated how she would feel without her breasts and with implants instead. She also knew that this was an aggressive tumour.

She understood better than anyone, because of her personal experience with her mum's premature death due to cancer, that her own premature death was a very realistic outcome. She was devastated at the idea of her children, like herself, not having a mother into their adulthood. She thought of Hannah, like herself, not having a mother when she got married and had children. She thought of her sons living their adult lives without their gentle, kind mum and her future grandchildren not having a grandmother.

Her specialists decided to remove the tumour as soon as possible while it was still quite small. She was booked in immediately for the surgery. It was just prior to Christmas, and she spent Christmas in the hospital alone. Her husband didn't visit her at all while she was in Melbourne, but her daughter visited a couple of times. She had a mastectomy, which was quickly followed by a reconstruction. It wasn't felt that radiotherapy was necessary, and she started chemotherapy as soon as she recovered from the surgery.

The hospital organised for her to stay in its nearby Women's Hostel for the months she was in Melbourne. She had a dreadful reaction to her first round of chemo, so the treatment had to be changed. The Women's Hostel was home to women from rural and regional areas with a variety of different needs: physical health, mental health and addiction. Emily was on high-dose pain medication, which was challenging when some of the women were being treated for opiate addictions. As a result, once she had recovered from the surgery and the reaction to the chemotherapy, she was discharged home.

Emily didn't want to go home. She felt supported and safe at the hostel. She was being looked after by a group of wonderful, caring women, both staff and residents. She had a glimpse of a life without the abuse she had experienced for decades. Her husband came to escort her back to Tasmania. He berated her throughout the trip. He told her that she was wasting his time, he had more important things to do, and she was causing him to miss a day at work. Not once did he ask how she was. This was a man who had vowed, as her husband, to care for her in sickness and in health.

Her chemotherapy was transferred from Melbourne to Hobart. It was miserable. She lost her sense of taste, her mouth was full of ulcers, and the nausea and vomiting were wretched. She wasn't eating, so she became quite malnourished and very weak. Emily was always slim but now she was gaunt and underweight. Even more seriously, her white blood cell count dropped dangerously low with each round. She was vulnerable to any kind of infectious disease in the community.

It was during her cancer experience that Emily felt closer to her mother than ever before. She could understand what she had been through and the impact on her body. She desperately wanted and needed her mum in the midst of this. Her father, whilst concerned about his eldest daughter, remained distant and uninvolved. Her sister stayed living in Brisbane after her university course. She was working and could only visit Emily sporadically. Of course, she was also very afraid of Emily's husband and didn't feel at all safe coming to visit.

By this time, Emily's children had all left home to study at various universities on the mainland. Her husband continued to work long hours, so Emily managed her chemotherapy journey alone. A close friend drove her to her appointments and generally made sure she was ok. After her last round of treatment, her white blood cell count was extremely low; she developed an infection and had a raging temperature. She managed to take herself to her local GP, who was so worried about her that he called an ambulance. Emily was admitted to the hospital in the late afternoon.

It was getting close to Christmas by now, twelve months on from her original diagnosis. The usual Christmas parties and festivities had begun. Emily's husband had been out every day and evening for weeks. The hospital staff called him to let him know Emily had been admitted. They had to leave a message as he didn't answer his phone. Eventually, hours later, he arrived at the hospital. He was drunk, loud and offensive and had to be asked to leave. That was the only time he visited her. She had to stay in an isolation room in the hospital for over a month whilst the medical staff endeavoured to control her infection. Eventually, they decided to medivac her back to Melbourne.

Emily remained in Melbourne for another few months, initially in hospital, followed by a couple of months at the Women's Hostel whilst she attended outpatient appointments and recovered. Unbeknownst to Emily, whilst she was in Melbourne, her husband told their children that he and Emily had separated. He told them that they had separated due to Emily's poor mental health and alcoholism and that she had been unfaithful. He controlled the narrative.

Emily continues to feel utterly betrayed by this. She firmly believes that if a couple separates, they need to tell the children together. Telling the children together gives them a coherent, unbiased and truthful story. When she was due to return home, her husband telephoned her and said he thought they should separate. She had no idea of the conversation he had with the children and assumed that once she got home, they would tell them together and make a plan.

Emily flew back to Tasmania and got a taxi from the airport. Once home, she was confused when she found out that her house keys didn't work. She went around to the back to try the other doors, but none of them would open. She knocked on the door so her husband could let her in. Instead, a woman came to the door, dressed in Emily's dressing gown. Her husband had already left for work. Emily was shocked and told the woman to let her in. The other woman refused and called Emily's husband instead. He rang the police and made a complaint that Emily was trying to break in; he told them they had separated, and she was causing a ruckus.

The police duly arrived. Emily tried to explain that it was her house and she had been in Melbourne having treatment for breast cancer. She told them that her name was on the mortgage and the homeownership documents. Of course, these documents were all inside the house, and they wouldn't let her in to access them. Emily only had the small bag of clothes and personal care items that she had taken to Melbourne with her a few months before. The police firmly told her to leave, or they would arrest her. They wouldn't even let her in the house to get more clothes and her car keys.

The history between Emily's parents was repeated in her own marriage. A husband who had frequent affairs and then, while she was managing cancer, moved his affair partner into the house. The only difference is that Emily's mum had died before her father brought another woman into the family home.

Emily called a friend to pick her up. As she re-grouped, she had to work out where she could go. She couldn't think of anywhere except the Women's Hostel that had been so supportive. She called them and they confirmed she could stay with them for a short time. Emily then had to organise to fly back to Melbourne the following day. She also decided that, having already taken extended sick leave from work, she needed to resign.

Emily stayed at the Hostel for a few weeks. They helped her apply for the Disability Support Pension, and she was eventually discharged into a flat they found for her. It was a horrible flat in a fairly unsafe part of the city, but it was all Emily could afford. Despite sharing a joint bank account, she was unable to access it. Her husband had spoken to the bank. He told them that Emily had severe mental health issues and shouldn't have access to any money without his approval. She had no financial support apart from the small amount of her salary she had saved and the Disability Support Pension. Whilst she was at the Hostel, she repeatedly attempted to have her husband send her belongings, including her precious photos and mementos of her mum, and to allow her to get her car. He refused.

THIRTEEN

Emily was scared and alone, stuck in a city she had no desire to live in. Her husband refused to engage with her. She desperately wanted to return to Sydney so she could be closer to her long-term friends and her father, but she didn't have enough money to afford rental prices or gather enough money for a deposit. She had been isolated from her children, her job, her finances, her friends and her support network, and now her husband was commencing divorce proceedings in the Family Court.

Emily pleaded with her abuser to provide some finances. Eventually, he agreed to pay the rent for a flat in Newcastle for a couple of months. He refused to pay rent for a flat in Sydney because it was, in his opinion, too expensive. At least in Newcastle, she could catch a train to Sydney to see her friends and family.

Emily had no job, and after such a significant cancer experience and poor mental health related to the trauma she had experienced, she began to drink again. On top of these issues, her children refused to see her, such was their father's power of persuasion about Emily's shortcomings. The solicitor he had engaged for the family court dispute was brutal. She desperately tried to stop drinking on multiple occasions and accessed professional help. She wanted to get back into the workforce, but her ill health, exhaustion, and stress from the legal proceedings were relentless and made it impossible.

She continued to appeal for him to send her belongings, including precious photos of her mother and some keepsakes from her. He continued to refuse. Emily had to find legal representation, and she had to spend all of her savings to do this. Nevertheless, the lawyer that Emily engaged was, in my opinion, at best biased against Emily due to her addiction issues or, at worst, incompetent.

Emily and her sister were both due to receive an inheritance from their grandfather's estate once their step-grandmother died. Given her significant age, they were both expecting it to be soon. Emily and I discussed this situation on multiple occasions. She was dreadfully worried that if her step-grandmother died prior to the Family Court matter being finalised, her abuser would make every effort to ensure the inheritance came to him as part of the settlement. Fortunately, that didn't eventuate, but it added to the stress Emily was already experiencing.

As is the norm with the Family Court, their dispute took several years to finalise. Emily's abuser once again engaged a top Barrister to represent him. Both parties were assessed by Family Court clinicians. Of course, Emily's abuser presented himself as a caring and devoted father who had suffered his wife's alcoholism for decades. He presented her as mentally unstable. Emily, of course, presented as stressed, mentally unwell and an alcoholic. Her abuser was believed; she wasn't.

Previously, I touched on the concept of the "*perpetrator's pattern of behaviour*" and how they may "*cause, interfere or exacerbate*" issues relating to the wellbeing of the victim-survivors. The Safe and Together Framework makes it clear that we must understand the "*Multiple Pathways to Harm*" that the perpetrator has engaged in.

Multiple pathways to harm bring together and make clear the impact of the patterns of behaviour perpetrators have used as a parenting choice. Whilst they may think their behaviour is only impacting the adult victim-survivor, it is essential that we understand their behaviour as a parenting choice, particularly when matters are before the Family Court. It is also essential that Family Court assessments are fully cognisant of the perpetrator's pattern of abuse and their individual multiple pathways to harm, particularly because there is a history within the Family Court of victim-survivors not being believed and perpetrators not being held accountable for their behaviour. Safe and Together's Multiple Pathways to Harm is explained in the following diagram:

Multiple Pathways to Harm

Perpetrator's Pattern
- Coercive control toward adult survivor
- Actions taken to harm children

Children's Trauma & Safety
- Victim of physical abuse
- Seeing, hearing or learning about the violence

Effect on Partner's Parenting
- Depression, PTSD, anxiety, substance abuse
- Loss of authority
- Energy goes to addressing perpetrator instead of children
- Interference with day to day routine and basic care

Effects on Family Ecology
- Loss of income
- Housing instability
- Loss of contact with extended family
- Educational and social disruptions

Harm to Child
- Behavioral, Emotional, Social, Educational
- Developmental
- Physical Injury

The following paragraphs draw the connection between the Multiple Pathways to Harm and Emily's specific situation, highlighted in bold.

When we consider Emily and her children, it is clear that the abuser used **patterns of coercive control** toward her. Whilst he did not physically harm the children, his habit of waking them up to see their aunt and their mother cowering on the floor whilst he berated his adult victims in front of them, hearing the violence, seeing the impact of it and listening to their father continually degrade their mother caused them **trauma**.

When we consider the effects on the **family's ecology,** his behaviour caused a **loss of income** as Emily wasn't able to work for significant periods of time. It caused **housing instability** and **educational and social disruptions** when he insisted on moving the family from Sydney to Launceston and then Hobart. The move to Tasmania caused the **children to lose contact** with their maternal extended family, and their subsequent move to Hobart impacted their contact with their paternal extended family.

When we consider the **impact of his pattern of behaviour on Emily's parenting,** he caused her **substance abuse.** She **lost her**

authority and emotional connection with the children because of his demeaning and belittling behaviour towards her. **She spent time and energy pacifying him** that she could have focussed on the children. His abuse **interfered with their day-to-day routine** and basic care, particularly when he prevented Emily's attempts at learning to drive but also due to her alcohol addiction and times in rehab. There can be no doubt that his pattern of behaviour caused harm to their children. None of this was considered in the assessments.

The Family Court of Australia has a troubling history when it comes to the protection of victim-survivors (adults and children). Frequently, children are forced to spend time with an abusive parent. Frequently, victim-survivors are forced to manage the perpetrator's behaviour post-separation due to Family Court orders. Frequently, abuse and violence continue after separation and divorce. Frequently, decisions regarding who the protective parent is are wrong, and the protective parent loses parental responsibility.

Jess Hill won three Our Watch Walkley awards for her investigations into domestic violence. She is the author of the book "Look What You Made Me Do" and has spent years reporting on and researching domestic violence. In 2019, she published an article in The Guardian about her investigations into The Family Court of Australia. It is worth quoting almost her entire article here for readers to appreciate the sustained issues[33].

When I first started hearing these stories, I didn't believe they were part of a pattern. Everyone knows someone who's had a shitty time in the family law system. Besides, I knew that this system was actually biased against fathers, not mothers. I believed then, like 43% of Australians, that vindictive mothers routinely lobbed abuse allegations at their ex-husbands to stop them seeing their children.

But then I started reading their court documents and the research.

In 2001, a joint study by the family court and the University of Sydney found that the family law system had "tilted more and more against women, either by accident or design". Even where serious

33 https://www.theguardian.com/commentisfree/2019/sep/19/i-believed-the-family-court-system-was-bias-against-fathers-then-i-found-the-rot-at-the-core-of-it?CMP=Share_iOSApp_Other

violence had been proven, it found, supervised contact with abusive fathers was becoming much more common.

In 2006, despite this noted tilt against women, and after three years of what then-legal associate Waleed Aly described as "an incessant and often intimidatory campaign by father's rights groups", the Howard government introduced new reforms to the Family Law Act. They were, on the face of it, reasonable – judges should apply a presumption of shared parental responsibility unless violence or abuse was an issue. But there was a catch: if a parent alleged abuse, they could be labelled a "hostile parent", unwilling to support shared parenting.

The punishment for hostile parents could be extreme: they not only ran the risk of losing custody of their children, they could be blocked from seeing or even speaking to them for months.

In 2007, Rae Kaspiew (now at the Australian Institute of Family Studies) found there were very limited circumstances in which a mother could challenge ongoing paternal involvement, "except in cases where the evidence of severe violence was clear-cut". In his report, former family court judge Richard Chisholm called this trap "the victim's dilemma", a position later articulated by former attorney general Robert McClelland: "Do I report family violence to the court and risk losing my children, or should I stay silent?"

*This change in attitude was made explicit in a 2007 judgment from Justice Tim Carmody (who was, for a brief and controversial period, Queensland's chief justice). It read: "**The consequences of denying contact between the abusive parent, usually the father, and the child may well be as serious as the risk of harm from abuse ... There is no presumption or a priori rule that even gross misbehaviour such as child sexual abuse ... puts up an insurmountable barrier in the way of having contact with a child victim.**"*

How does this attitude influence the outcome of a custody dispute? Take this case, for example, from 2010. A father already on the sex offenders register for possessing child abuse images was fighting for equal care of his daughters, aged eight and 10. The mother was requesting he have supervised daytime contact only. Their eldest daughter had told child-protection workers that she loved her father and didn't want to upset him but wasn't comfortable staying over at his house, particularly on her own. When asked why, she referred them back to what she'd told the police but became "extremely distressed" when pressed to elaborate. She repeatedly pleaded with child-protection workers not to repeat what she'd said to her father.

In his judgment, Justice Robert Benjamin of the Hobart family court accepted that the father had demonstrated "inappropriate" affection towards his daughter. He also believed the mother's allegation that several years earlier, she had seen the father with an erection, leaning over and touching his five-year-old stepdaughter while her pyjama pants were down, and he accepted that the mother delayed reporting it for years because she was afraid of the father.

The justice also found that the father had been intimidating during the marriage and was "manipulative and disingenuous" in his evidence. Despite all this, the justice ordered that the daughters spend alternate weekends and half the school holidays with their father. Overnight stays were to be supervised by an "adult friend" of the father to "address" the elder daughter's nervousness, and the daughters should share a room for "mutual support". Everyone knows someone who's had a shitty time in the family law system.

In 2012, after three research studies found that victims of abuse were not being protected in the family law system, then-attorney general Nicola Roxon announced another set of reforms to the Family Law Act – essentially, attempting to undo the harm done by the Howard reforms. Under the current Family Law Act, judges are to prioritise the protection of children "from physical or psychological harm and from being subjected to, or exposed to, abuse, neglect or family violence". This is to be a higher priority than the "benefit to the child of having a meaningful relationship with both parents".

But even with this substantial change to the legislation, the same stories persist. They land in my inbox every week. The anti-violence campaigner Rosie Batty even told me that were it not for the family law system, she would hardly have any victims contacting her. Prominent doctors have confided in me their horror at what they see happening to their patients in the system – especially to the children.

In 2016, in the peer-reviewed legal journal Laws, Griffith University criminologist Samantha Jeffries wrote that in family court judgments, domestic violence was "ignored or minimised, reconstructed as inconsequential" or passed off as mutual violence, where both parents are equally at fault.

More chilling, however, were findings Jeffries (and others) published in the UNSW Law Journal that same year.

This was a study on family reports – one of the most important pieces of evidence in a family law hearing – written by psychiatrists, social workers and psychologists, assessing the family dynamic and, commonly, evaluating allegations of abuse.

Legal practitioners openly stated that they knew which family report writers to go to if they were representing a perpetrator. Said one: "When I worked in private practice we would look for report writers who don't do that level of investigation, who don't report on the violence because that was in our client's [the perpetrator's] interest."

This is the evidence. This is the rot at the core of our family law system. Yes, many fathers have a terrible time in the family law system. There is no excuse for an innocent man being deprived of access to his children. But there is a pyramid of harm.

Like Jess Hill, the ABC's Heidi Davoren has recently reported on the systemic issues within the Family Court which harm victim-survivors[34]. *"...horrific, traumatic, broken, unethical — these are some of the words Australians have used to describe their experience in the family court system".* Note: Both David Mandel from the Safe and Together Institute and I were interviewed individually for this story. It seems that five years later, there continue to be systemic issues within the Family Court.

Time after time, I observed these issues myself when I was a practitioner in the field. I am the lead author of the internationally recognised Keeping Kids in Mind parenting course, specifically developed for parents who are engaged in chronic conflict post-separation. The course was developed by a team of experts in their fields: mediation, child development, parenting, and relationship counselling. It is the only externally evaluated multi-session course

---

34 https://www.abc.net.au/news/2024-09-06/family-court-family-violence-training-david-mandel/104183698?utm_campaign=abc_news_web&utm_content=link&utm_medium=content_shared&utm_source=abc_news_web

addressing these issues. I have worked with close to a thousand parents and facilitated training and clinical supervision for hundreds of practitioners over the 15 years since the program was developed. Stories like those described by Jess Hill, Heidi Davoren, and Rosie Batty are ones I have heard weekly. These are not exceptions to the norm. They are the norm.

This situation and these decisions play heavily on the minds of practitioners, social workers, psychologists, and mediators. We talk a lot in the social science field about vicarious trauma and moral injury. Supporting our clients who are entrenched in the family law system and trying to manage significant danger can sometimes feel overwhelming. Our frustration is enormous, and we, like our clients, are helpless in influencing the system. Generally speaking, thinking about the examples that Jess Hill, Heidi Davoren, and other passionate and committed journalists speak about and specifically Emily's situation, regularly makes me despair. I cannot understand how human beings purposely and knowingly put the lives of children and protective parents even more at risk. Navigating these emotions and experiences on an almost daily basis is what causes practitioners to experience Vicarious Trauma, and being completely helpless to do anything about it leads us to a place of Moral Injury. Navigating these emotions when it comes to my closest friend is almost impossible.

On a positive note, the Family Court is undergoing training in the Safe and Together Framework. Whilst this is an encouraging move, the impact of legal professionals disregarding domestic violence is still far too entrenched. As we can see in Jess Hill's article, some solicitors actively seek out family report writers and clinicians who either don't understand domestic violence, don't know how to assess for it or willfully ignore it. Similarly, Independent Children's Lawyers (ICLs) are not specially trained in child development or domestic violence. There are far too many examples where ICLs have not advocated appropriately for the children they are supposed to be representing because they lack this specialist training. In my opinion, these professionals have no business practising in the field of family law. Their actions actively increase danger and are completely unethical. Within the current adversarial family law system, if a solicitor speaks about "winning" for their client, then the only individuals who actually lose are the children.

It is not just the Australian Family Court system where these issues exist. Similar entrenched biases and issues are reported in numerous Western countries, including the UK, the USA and various European countries. In my opinion, all Family Courts across all jurisdictions need to be trained in Safe and Together. Like Australia, the UK has already started implementing the framework. It is far too early to tell whether this will make any difference to judgments, but Emily and I sincerely hope it will. Currently, unfortunately, the impact appears to be minimal.

Angharad Candlin

FOURTEEN

The Family Court process was appalling. Her husband stood before the court, dressed in expensive suits with his Barrister and solicitor. He was articulate, confident and friendly. He was seemingly highly educated (he had continued to lie about his increasing academic qualifications) and middle class with a long and senior career in local government. He told lie after lie about Emily. He maintained that the head injury, decades before, was still severely impacting her and was the cause of her mental ill health and alcoholism. The court didn't request any evidence to support this narrative, and Emily's solicitor failed to challenge it. It could easily have been disproved with affidavits from her medical team and employment records.

The Family Consultant assessed the family. Emily talked about the decades of domestic violence. Her assertions weren't followed up. She simply wasn't believed. Instead, a picture was painted of an unreliable, mentally ill and alcoholic woman. A woman who hadn't cared for her children adequately. A woman who didn't have the capacity to care for herself and needed her life and finances to be managed. The whole court system, including Emily's own solicitor, colluded with the perpetrator as to the cause of Emily's ill health and addiction issues.

Ultimately, the judge determined that the assets be shared "fairly" and that Emily should keep her car. In reality, Emily received virtually nothing. Her abuser refused to comply with the orders. When they were discussing what items within the house were to be shared, Emily was adamant that she wanted her personal items, keepsakes from her mum, her large collection of books, her clothes and personal items and her pictures. She was clear that she didn't want the oversized (and now somewhat old and shabby) sofas because they wouldn't fit in her new home. Instead, he kept everything she requested and paid for a removalist to deliver the two sofas to Emily's flat, and she had to pay someone to take them away. She certainly got no proceeds from the sale of their high-value house, her car or share of significant superannuation. Her "settlement" came to about $300,000. Even more devastating, Emily's money was put into a trust, and she couldn't access it. The court deemed that her now ex-husband was best placed to manage it. Emily's solicitor didn't object.

Once more, despite the divorce, Emily's abuser was able to control her financially. Victim-survivors know that separation and divorce will not stop the abuse. It is the reason many victim-survivors don't leave. If they have younger children, they know that their children will be forced to have contact with an abusive parent, and it is highly likely, given the myriad cases that have gone before, that the perpetrator will weaponise the Family Court. The result so often is that the children are removed from the protective parent, placed with the perpetrator, and orders are made to restrict contact between the children and the victim-survivor who has been misrepresented as a perpetrator.

There are two phrases that are all too frequently used to misrepresent victim-survivors. The first is Parental Alienation Syndrome, and the second is Stockholm Syndrome. Both need to be addressed.

In recent years, there has been a growing call to reject Parental Alienation Syndrome. JS Meier[35] provides a concise history of the term. *"Parental Alienation Syndrome (PAS) was invented by Richard Gardner in the 1980s to explain what he considered to be an epidemic of child sexual abuse allegations in custody litigations. Gardner claimed, with no empirical basis, that the vast majority of such allegations are false but were fabricated by vengeful or pathological mothers. Credible and extensive empirical research has demonstrated that the assumptions underpinning PAS, including that child sexual abuse allegations are rampant and generally false, are themselves entirely false."*

---

35 https://vawnet.org/sites/default/files/materials/files/2016-09/AR_
    PASUpdate.pdf

She goes on to say, *"This (recent federally funded) research confirms that those who do not have an in-depth understanding of domestic violence also tend to label abuse allegations alienation and rarely identify abuse as a serious concern. Sadly, alienation labelling has also entered child welfare agency practices, who frequently discount and sometimes even turn against mothers who report child abuse by a father, particularly in the context of custody or visitation litigation."*

There is a plethora of scientific research about parental alienation. Generally speaking, parental alienation certainly can happen; however, the term is often misused. Meland E. et al[36] clearly explain the five criteria for making a positive assessment of parental alienation. Crucially, one of them is *"the alienated parent has not subjected the child to abuse or neglect."*

These criteria are overlooked in a remarkably high percentage of cases where parental alienation is claimed. The research tells us that both men and women equally utilise parental alienation; however, if domestic violence is not adequately understood and assessed, we have to be cautious about ever using the term.

In reality, in situations of coercive control, the perpetrator will assert they are the victim of parental alienation, when in fact, it is the perpetrator of violence who is alienating the victim-survivor. In Emily's situation, we can see that her abuser systematically alienated Emily from her children, and in the following chapter, we will see how that continues even to this day.

It is essential to understand the parental alienation criteria within the context of domestic violence. Children are harmed by domestic violence regardless of whether they have directly been neglected or abused. The abuse of a parent is itself the abuse of a child. We need to consider this in the context of the Family Law system. If the system itself is not able to accurately assess domestic violence, then a diagnosis of parental alienation cannot ever be made with confidence.

---

36 Parental alienation - a valid experience? Scandinavian Journal of Public Health 2023 Apr 23;52(5):598–606 https://pmc.ncbi.nlm.nih.gov/articles/PMC11292963/

It is reassuring that some professionals working within the Family Law system are being trained in Safe and Together, but many are not. Until all professionals involved in the Family Law system are adequately trained in Safe and Together, adult and child victim-survivors will continue to be abused by the system itself. Unfortunately, in Australia, the training of Family Law professionals is happening at a snail's pace. In many other western jurisdictions, there is no systematic training of Family Law professionals around domestic violence, and parental alienation continues to be used in an alarming number of cases without question.

The second term that is frequently used within a domestic violence narrative is Stockholm Syndrome. The syndrome is generally used to describe a situation where a victim of violence forms a bond with the perpetrator. Stockholm Syndrome was coined following an attempted bank robbery and hostage situation in Stockholm, Sweden, in August 1973. Briefly, four bank employees were held hostage for six days.

Dr Allan Wade is a respected Canadian domestic violence researcher and clinician who, years later, spent days interviewing the survivor after whom the term was coined. Over the six days, the hostages became increasingly scared of how the police were going to respond to the situation. The police pointed their guns through a window at the bank robbers even when the hostages were in the line of fire. The bank robbers actually protected the hostages from being fired upon by the police. The police negotiators became increasingly hostile and agitated whilst the bank robbers remained calm. It was a phone call with the then-Swedish Prime Minister that cemented their terror. One of the hostages told the Prime Minister that they were all well looked after by the hostage takers and trusted they would not harm them. In contrast, the Prime Minister confirmed he would not negotiate with the bank robbers even if it meant that the hostages would die.

The bank employees, with very good reason, felt safer with the hostage takers than the police, given the Prime Minister's acknowledgment they would die and the hostility of the police aggravating the situation. They knew that if they were to have a chance of surviving, they had to develop a relationship with the hostage takers so that they were seen as individual people, not just expendable pawns in a deadly situation.

When the siege finally ended, the hostages were brought out, unnecessarily, on stretchers. None of them had been harmed. The woman who prompted the invention of the term Stockholm Syndrome did not want to be taken out on a stretcher. She wanted to walk out as an indication of her resilience. Paramedics and police insisted she go out on the stretcher, but as a testament to her strength of character, she refused to lie down and sat up on the stretcher. This was not looked upon kindly by the police, who saw it as another example of the victim's collusion with the hostage takers. In reality, it was an act of resistance against the police and Prime Minister, who had risked the hostages' lives far more than their captors.

The term Stockholm Syndrome was made up on the spot during a media interview following the release of the hostages by a Swedish Psychiatrist, Nils Bejerot. He said that the victims had been brainwashed by their captors and, in the next breath, called it *"Norrmalmstorgssyndromet"* after the city Square where the siege took place. It was later renamed Stockholm Syndrome for ease of use outside Sweden. The syndrome has not been accepted by the Psychiatric profession and is not listed in the Diagnostic and Statistical Manual of Mental Disorders (DSM). Nevertheless, it continues to be used. This has to stop, and we all need to take responsibility for not using the term.

Ironically, if anyone suffered from something like what is understood as Stockholm Syndrome, it was the captors. In an interview, Olsson[37] (one of the hostage takers) explained that he was the one, in fact, who formed a bond with his victims: *"It was the hostages' fault. They did everything I told them to. If they hadn't, I might not be here now. Why didn't any of them attack me? They made it hard to kill. They made us go on living together day after day, like goats, in that filth. There was nothing to do but get to know each other"*.

The use of the term Stockholm Syndrome is pervasive in the community in an attempt to explain why victim-survivors of domestic

---

37 https://www.bbc.com/news/magazine-22447726

violence don't leave the relationship. Respectfully, those who are not specially trained in response to domestic violence generally do not comprehend the nuances of coercive control. They do not understand that staying with the perpetrator is often the safest and most rational option both for the survivor and their children.

If an adult victim-survivor leaves, they know that the perpetrator will use the court system to their advantage, with the very real risk that the children will be removed from them, the protective parent, and placed with the abusive parent. They stay to better protect their children. They stay because they don't have anywhere to go. They stay because they don't have access to finances. They stay because they know the perpetrator will stalk them and/or their family. They stay because they are concerned family members and/or friends will be assaulted. They stay because they know the family pet will be killed. They stay because they can't trust the police or the court systems, Criminal or Family. They stay because when a victim-survivor leaves, they know they are more vulnerable to being murdered. They stay because they know the perpetrator will murder their children and then kill themselves.

FIFTEEN

Emily felt like she had been unceremoniously dumped in Newcastle by her abusive husband. She had no support network there, and she didn't know anyone. She didn't have a GP or a counsellor. She was out of work, and, given her vulnerable mental health, wasn't really in a position to find employment. Nevertheless, her resilience allowed her to rise to the challenge of establishing herself. She found a women's support network that became her life support.

Encouraged by me and various other friends, and with the support of the women's network, she found another solicitor who fought in the courts for her abuser to be removed as the trustee. Whilst the court refused to give Emily the power to manage her own finances, the trusteeship was transferred to her three children. So now her future was in the hands of her children, who had been fed lies from their father about their mother. For every single cent she needed, over and above her disability support pension, she had to go cap in hand to her children. Emily's abuser retracted the financial support he had been providing to pay the rent on her flat. He refused to let her collect the car she had bought for herself or even have someone collect it for her. Instead, he sold it and kept the proceeds for himself.

Her children were all coming to the end of their university courses. Ellis' graduation was around the corner; Hannah's and Patrick's were not far behind, and Hugh was still studying. Emily always spoke to me with significant pride about all of her children. At the time, she was particularly excited and focused on Ellis' graduation. She was and is so proud of him. She remembers the details with clarity and delight.

A year later was Hannah's graduation. Hannah contacted her mum and told her she didn't want her to attend her graduation. She didn't want her mum to *"show her up or turn up drunk"*. Something Emily would never have done. She was devastated that this precious moment was taken from her. It is clear to me that Hannah is repeating things she has heard her father say for years.

Patrick's graduation was next, followed by Hugh's. Emily was relieved and happy that they both wanted her there. Like Ellis' graduation, she remembers the details precisely. It was becoming increasingly clear, however, that her abuser was continuing to use coercive control, but this time, he was weaponising his own children against their mother, particularly Hannah. When one parent uses their child, irrespective of the child's age, to cause harm to the protective parent, they are abusing their children.

Emily and Hannah had always had a close relationship. Emily regularly made sure that they had time together. Hannah had been quite ill during her adolescence, and Emily had fought hard for her to receive the medical care she needed. Hannah wanted and needed her mum during these months. Emily was sober and sat with Hannah for hours in the hospital, holding her when she was frightened about the medical procedure she was going to need. Hannah's rejection and the loss of this precious relationship have cut Emily to her core.

Emily eventually decided that she couldn't live in Newcastle any more, and given the settlement had been finalised and the trust transferred to her children, she looked for a flat to buy outright. She didn't want to ever again be reliant on anyone for the roof over her head. She also didn't want to use all of the money from the settlement, so she looked at former public housing that had been released for sale. She knew she couldn't afford Sydney, but she could just about afford some areas of the Central Coast. On the Central Coast, she was only 45 minutes by train to the northern suburbs of Sydney, where she had grown up and where some of her lifelong friends and father still resided.

She found a cheap flat for sale on the edge of a housing commission estate. It was a huge comedown from what she was used to, but it could be hers. She went about asking her children to release the funds to buy the flat. They agreed, and Ellis organised the purchase. It took longer than usual because of the complexity of buying a government-owned property. As it turns out, this was a blessing in disguise.

This all happened in the few years prior to the COVID-19 pandemic. The most devastating event, though, was still to come. Emily received the news that her beloved friend Jen had taken her own life. Emily was completely heartbroken by this news. She knew that Jen had been troubled by events in her life, including the violent rape she had experienced at the hands of Emily's abuser. She felt guilty and responsible for Jen's assault. She was overwhelmed with her own grief and grief for Jen's son. This was to be the tipping point for Emily's mental health.

After moving to Newcastle, Emily had met another man with whom she slowly started a friendship, which became a romantic relationship. He seemed nice enough. Unsurprisingly, I had reservations. But as it turned out, whilst he has his shortcomings, he is nothing like Emily's abuser.

Emily and I had been planning a time for me to visit in the coming days when, late one evening, I got a call from her new partner. He was extremely worried about Emily. He said she was pacing around the flat and not making any sense. I agreed with him that he should call Emily's GP as soon as possible, and I reassured him that I would come first thing the following morning.

It took a couple of hours to drive to Emily's flat from my home, so I arrived mid-morning. Her GP had already visited, and her opinion was that Emily needed to be involuntarily admitted into a residential mental health unit. She arranged for Emily to have a home visit from the mental health crisis team. When I arrived, Emily was clearly in the midst of psychosis. She was expressing paranoia and was terribly confused. She was suspicious of her new partner, who had locked the front door and wouldn't let her leave. He had locked the front door because he was worried she would harm herself. In response, Emily called her son Patrick and told him that she was being held hostage in her flat. Of course, Patrick was desperately worried, so he called the police to carry out a welfare check.

Emily looked incredibly relieved when she saw me. Here was one of her closest and oldest friends. Having rapidly assessed what was going on, I held her face in my hands and said, *"Do you know me?*" "*Yes*", Emily replied. "*Do you trust me?*" "*Yes,*" Emily replied. "*Then I am going to stay with you, and we are going to get through this together.*" I will never forget that interaction. As a friend, I was desperate for her, but I knew at that moment that Emily needed me to be both her friend and a psychologist.

She calmed a little, and I asked her partner to make a cup of tea for us both. I am known for saying there is nothing quite as healing as a cup of tea, especially in a crisis. Emily sat on the floor at my feet, and I stroked her hair while we were having our cups of tea. The on-call psychiatrist arrived and agreed that Emily needed to be admitted for residential psychiatric treatment. Emily didn't have private health insurance, so the community mental health team needed to find a bed for her in a public hospital. That was going to take some time. The psychiatrist prescribed medication to help Emily manage and organised for one of the mental health social workers to come.

Once Emily had taken the medication, she settled and went for a lie down on her bed. I followed, and we lay there chatting a little bit. It was then that the police arrived, following up on Patrick's phone call. They checked, and Emily was okay, so I explained the situation. I also explained who I was and asked them to let Patrick know that I was with Emily so he could be reassured his mum was safe.

The mental health social worker arrived a little later, and she stayed with us whilst we waited to find out where there was an available bed. She was amazing. Incredibly calm, caring and safe. She reassured Emily's partner, and she was a beautiful support to all of us. At one point, I remember chatting to her in the kitchen and telling her that this isn't Emily. This isn't my gorgeous, intelligent, kind friend. She said she could tell just from the way Emily spoke that she wasn't herself. Although, at the time, I didn't know the details about the years of hell that Emily had endured, I knew enough to tell her that Emily had been subjected to years of abuse. At that moment, she did the kindest and most meaningful thing I think could ever have been done. She took me in her arms, hugged me and said, "*He broke her.*" I wept for my friend and said, "*Yes, he did.*"

This man purposefully, over decades, stripped my friend piece by piece of all that she was and all that she could be. He chose to take another human being and degrade her, abuse her, violate her, alienate her children and then toss her aside once he had finished with her. He not only broke her, but he smashed her into a million pieces so that she could never be put back together again. He completely destroyed her life.

Eventually, the ambulance arrived to transport Emily to the residential psychiatric unit. The social worker and I went downstairs with her, and I watched as they secured her in the ambulance and drove away with her. I have absolutely no words to describe the agony of that moment. Knowing this, the social worker silently put her arm around me and made sure I was ok.

It was early evening by then, and I didn't feel I could safely drive all the way home, so I rang a good friend who lives on the NSW Central Coast and asked if I could stay with them for the night. They were wonderful. My friend is an Occupational Therapist and has worked with mentally unwell patients, so she knew exactly what I had been through that day. Without asking me anything, she and her husband poured me a drink and ordered pizza. We sat outside in their garden, talking about mundane things until I couldn't stay awake any longer. I fell into their spare bed and slept like a log. After breakfast I drove home, all the time wondering how Emily was. Two weeks later, she called me from the psychiatric unit. She was well, the care she received was second to none, and a few weeks later, she was discharged and referred to the community mental health team. She has never had another episode.

A few months after this crisis, she could move into her new flat. Her new partner moved with her, and finally, after years of pleading, her abuser sent her mother's keepsakes and some of her belongings to her, but not her clothes, her treasured books or pictures. Recently, we were talking about this issue. Emily mentioned that she didn't have any photos of the children when they were little. I was thrown by that. I had no idea that he was so cruel as to deny her photos of her children. Fortunately, I have some and told her, in fact, during the conversation, I was looking at a framed school photo of Emily (as a teacher) with her children. Emily became teary when she heard she could finally have photos of her children. Something so small was denied to her by this man.

I offered to drive down to Tasmania and pick up the rest of her things for her. I knew that her abuser wouldn't dare do anything to me and, in fact, would be scared to encounter my wrath. In the end, Emily declined the offer. She just didn't want to have to deal with him and was afraid he would alienate the children from her even more.

Emily went about settling in and creating a home. We talked one day, and she said all she wanted was a little home with a little garden she could potter in overlooking the sea. She finally had it. It was a small dream for someone with the potential for such a big future when we first met. Once again, she set about accessing support, medical, mental health and addiction services. She joined a cooperative of women who spent time creating various kinds of craftwork. Finally, it seemed she could exhale.

SIXTEEN

There is a quotation I heard when I was participating in the practitioner training for the Circle of Security Parenting Program. Kent Hoffman told us the story of his former Psychology Professor, who said a sentence he has never forgotten; *"Every person you will ever meet has infinite worth"*. It is his North Star, and it has become my own North Star.

Years later, I was facilitating a training session for a parenting program my team and I developed for parents whose children have been removed into statutory care. At the end of the two-day training, we use the above quote. A participant quizzed us on whether this quote could possibly be true in a world where so much apparent evil exists. She specifically had in mind perpetrators of domestic violence. *"Absolutely,"* I said confidently. No infant is born evil or "less than" anyone else. In fact, the idea that someone is worth less than someone else is abhorrent.

Some people have mental ill health. Some people have endured traumatic events, traumatic childhoods, or generational trauma. Some people have drug and alcohol addictions. Some people have grown up in violence and now use violence themselves. None of them are evil. Nevertheless, it is important to note that whilst everyone has inherent value and some people have had terrible things happen to them, a person's deplorable behaviour can never be excused.

For too long, perpetrators of violence have been viewed simply as "bad" by the general community and even some mental health and community practitioners. As a result, they have not received the services they desperately need in order to change their behaviour. If we are to effectively deal with this epidemic of domestic violence across the world, then we must engage with perpetrators of violence. We must hold perpetrators to account, not by condemning and shaming them but by engaging them in a respectful conversation about their values. Compassionately challenging them when their behaviour and values don't match up and, when necessary, utilising the legal system to impose proportionate consequences.

Historically, the majority of government funding has been directed almost solely towards supporting victim-survivors. It has never been remotely adequate to address the scale of the problem. However, it is further limited in effectiveness by the failure to address the issues related to perpetrators of violence. If we don't deal with the source of the problem, we could spend trillions of dollars on domestic violence with no impact whatsoever.

According to the organisation No To Violence, there are currently 16 funded Men's Behaviour Change Programs in NSW. For many years, there were only five across the whole state, and three of them were in the Sydney Metro area. In Victoria, there are 30. In South Australia, there are 12, three in Queensland, two each in Tasmania, the ACT and the Northern Territory and one in Western Australia. In Australia, there are stringent minimum standards that organisations must meet in order to facilitate Men's Behaviour Change groups.

Men's Line Australia[38] has a host of resources to support men across all areas of life. They can be contacted to source accredited Men's Behaviour Change Programs in each state.

In the UK, Canada, Europe and the USA, by way of comparison, there are no clear mechanisms for counting the number of groups, no clear and easily obtained minimum standards and minimal or no funding. The European Network for Work with Perpetrators of Domestic Violence provides information about the countries that are involved in behaviour change groups, but data on the numbers of funded organisations is very difficult to find. Despite Australia's leading edge on minimum standards for Men's Behaviour Change groups and clarity in reporting, the numbers of funded organisations are woefully inadequate.

---

38 https://mensline.org.au/about-us/useful-links-and-support/

The community services organisation Drummond Street, in Victoria, offers a Behaviour Change group for female, trans and gender-diverse perpetrators of violence. There are virtually no other services that are similar to Drummond Street's perpetrator program. Clearly, the whole world has a problem engaging with domestic violence perpetrators of any gender. Unless our entire community commits to engaging with perpetrators, the plight of victim-survivors like Emily will continue.

Perpetrator behaviour change programs, whilst a significant tool, are only one element in the solution to address domestic violence. If we are to effectively deal with domestic violence, it must be a whole of community approach.

This book is not an attempt to analyse the very specific complexities within domestic violence. There are many reports available that outline the risks of domestic violence to First Nations, LGBTQI, religious communities and those with disabilities. Rather, with this book, I have endeavoured to provide a framework to understand, broadly speaking, the impact and nuances of domestic violence, particularly coercive control, whilst undertaking a "*deep dive*" into one woman's experience of violence.

In Australia, federal and state governments are starting to address the inadequate funding for work with perpetrators. Nevertheless, individuals or families may never be referred to a service specialising in domestic violence. It behoves the government, business, community, health, legal, criminal, faith and education sectors to be trained specifically in how to recognise and respond to domestic violence, how to engage with perpetrators and how to effectively support victim-survivors.

Practitioners who are not trained in domestic violence responses can unwittingly create even more danger for victim-survivors. This is not to say all support agencies should become behaviour change specialists; indeed this would be even more problematic and minimise the importance of the rigorous training, expertise and experience required for such a role. Given the pervasive nature of domestic violence, it is guaranteed that individuals who work in people-facing roles will be alongside victim-survivors and perpetrators of violence whether or not they have identified themselves as such. There is a responsibility for all staff, irrespective of their role or sector, to be educated and trained in how to effectively respond to domestic violence.

Generally speaking, professionals who are untrained in domestic violence responses but are involved with families where domestic violence is being perpetrated may do one of four things: completely miss the nuances of a domestic violence presentation, actively intervene but in a way that misses or minimises the danger, misidentify the perpetrator or refuse to work with the perpetrator as part of a family dynamic. Those who come into contact with a couple or family where domestic violence is present must understand the signs and dangers of coercive control and be equipped to respond.

This is why Safe and Together is such a crucial tool for addressing domestic violence. Experts have created educational resources for the whole community in evidence-based and effective strategies to address domestic violence. It is why I am such a strong proponent of the framework.

Over recent years, the public outcry against domestic violence has become increasingly loud. Unfortunately, women are doing most of the shouting. As I said earlier, violence is gendered. The lack of male voices calling for other men to be accountable has been deafening in its silence. The organisation Our Watch has some incredibly helpful resources and conducts research into this area. I encourage everyone to go to their website and engage with their resources. In November 2024, their research indicated that 80% of men want to do something about domestic violence, but 43% of those men don't know what to do.

Some of the issues that I have heard from men about this statistic is that they feel so overwhelmed and ashamed by the values, beliefs and behaviour of a minority of men that they feel paralysed. Other men have said that because men are victims too, they feel invisible, and the amount of airtime given to female victims of domestic violence is unfair. Other men are not aware of the lengths that women go to in their everyday lives to protect themselves. Some are genuinely fearful of retribution if they do make a stand. Generally speaking, many men simply don't know what to do, so they do nothing.

Jackson Katz is an academic who has spent almost his whole adult life working against gendered violence. He has particularly engaged boys and men around bystander behaviour. He teaches men strategies to intervene in a safe way when they see or hear misogynistic conversations or behaviour. An easy-to-read toolkit is his latest book, "Every Man: why violence against women is a men's issue." 2025, Penguin[39].

There are many simple things men can do to change the course of domestic violence and actively choose not to be a bystander:

- They can have a quiet word with their friends if they hear disrespectful, gender-based language being used.
- They can refuse to laugh at sexist jokes.
- They can walk away if disrespectful conversations are occurring.
- They can purposely engage men in conversations about values.
- They can report workplace harassment if they see it or hear about it.
- They can believe their female family, friends or colleagues if they tell them they have been harassed.
- They can support and champion their female colleagues.
- They can call out workplace gender inequities if they become aware of them.
- They can commit to not perpetuating workplace gender inequities.
- They can commit to being loving, involved and committed fathers who are empathic with their children but also hold them to account for disrespectful behaviour.
- They can hold schools or out-of-school activities to account if they see gender inequities.

---

39 https://www.penguin.com.au/books/every-man-9780241672662

- They can raise concerns about organised activities that sexualise girls or push boys to be tough.
- They can make a stand against pornography and prostitution.
- They can model respectful, kind and loving relationships with their partners.
- They can share resources about domestic violence in their workplaces, on social media, and in their extracurricular activities.
- They can overtly join in the public outcry against domestic violence.
- If they see abusive behaviour from one person to another in a public place, they can silently stand between the aggressor and the victim, forming a physical barrier whilst not engaging with the aggressor.
- They can ensure their female friends/family get home or to taxis safely.
- They can calmly intervene if a man is "coming onto" a woman and not responding to her protestations.
- If they see violence occurring, they can call the police immediately.

Recently, I supported a victim-survivor of domestic violence to report a breach of an AVO. The breach did not come directly to her; it came in the form of a third person. It was not a threat of violence, but it was a message that those of us who understand coercive control could immediately see as a threat. The underlying message was, "*I can get to you*". It was enough to create terror and panic within the victim-survivor.

The two of us attended the local police station. The same Local Area Command had responded to the horrific act of violence about 18 months previously, resulting in charges, the AVO and a subsequent court case. A cursory look at their database would have provided the information the local duty constable required. We also had a copy of the AVO.

We described what had happened in terms of the breach. He asked if we had evidence. We said no. It was on the phone of the person who had received the breach and the phone of the perpetrator. He said he couldn't do anything without evidence because it was hearsay. I explained that the victim (who was now so distressed she was finding it hard to speak) had seen the text messages, so it wasn't hearsay. He reiterated that the police couldn't do anything without evidence, and besides, no real threat had been made, so it wasn't a breach.

I explained to him the new coercive control laws. I explained to him the man on the bus theory that something that seems banal to him or me is actually a threat in the context of domestic violence. I suggested he should contact the third party or indeed the perpetrator and he could access the evidence for himself. He half-heartedly said he would call the third party. A week later, nothing had been done, so I followed up. He said he'd called, but there had been no answer. The victim-survivor moved interstate two weeks later and has kept her location secret from everyone except two close friends, myself and one family member.

When, despite extensive training, police officers who come into contact with domestic violence every day cannot understand veiled threats of violence and do not respond appropriately; when they cannot effectively assess victims and perpetrators; when members of the public have to coach them in how to do their job - it is no wonder rates of domestic violence are through the roof.

When the health, education, criminal and legal systems use racial, cultural identity and gender stereotypes as their yardstick for intervention, refugees, migrants, LGBTQI and First Nations peoples will continue to be marginalised and oppressed.

When practitioners working with the community are not trained in effective, evidence-based domestic violence responses, victim-survivors and perpetrators alike will not be supported.

When officers of the family court consistently make orders that put victim-survivors of domestic violence in even more danger, women and children will continue to be murdered.

When judges in the criminal court make orders that are wholly inadequate, despite concrete and proven evidence of a pattern of violent behaviour over the years, the community will never be safe.

When women are falsely diagnosed as having a psychiatric disorder, or being hysterical, or are accused of parental alienation because they have endured decades of abuse and have finally said enough or because they have been labelled as having failed to protect their children who have been removed, the blame and responsibility for domestic violence will continue to sit with victim-survivors and perpetrators will never be held to account.

When governments over decades do not invest in perpetrator-primary prevention programs, domestic violence will never end.

When children and adolescents are disregarded as primary victim-survivors of domestic violence and don't receive support, then their mental health will be significantly impacted.

When boys and men who use violence are shamed and not supported, then their use of violence will escalate.

When individuals in government perpetrate abuse and are not held to account, perpetrators are effectively given a free pass to continue to use violence.

When faith leaders continue to uphold the myth that "*men are the head of the house*", that women should submit to men and that women cannot be faith leaders, women will continue to be gaslit, be unsafe within their spiritual communities and be in danger at home.

When the tabloid media continue to report domestic violence as a one-off incident, the community will never learn about the nuanced and insidious pattern of coercive control.

When the epidemic of easily accessible violent pornography remains unchecked, boys and girls will have a completely false narrative of what a loving relationship and consensual sex actually are.

When children have unfettered access to dangerous content online, their worlds will continue to be shattered.

When adults allow children and teenagers to use misogynistic/ misandrist or abusive or disrespectful language and when schools and parents do not encourage critical thinking or challenge offensive behaviours, children will grow up to be disrespectful and abusive adults.

When parents protect their children when they have been disrespectful, violent or abusive and bully teachers or others who are trying to hold children accountable, they are part of the problem.

When schools do not address bullying and do not actively engage in open and reparative justice between children, children grow up into adults who perpetrate abuse.

When fathers and men adhere to stereotypical gender roles and when mothers and women don't call out the disrespectful behaviour of children and adolescents, they are perpetuating the problem.

When babies, toddlers and young children are conditioned to behave like *"little girls"* and *"little boys"*, we will perpetuate the gender stereotypes that underpin domestic violence.

When the community says *"Boys will be boys"* or passes comments on what girls are wearing and says they were *"asking for it"*, girls and women will continue to be sexually assaulted.

When boys and men do not understand that unless it is an enthusiastic yes, rape will continue to occur.

When child sexual abuse is misreported as an *"underage sexual relationship"*, then children will continue to be sexually abused.

When women don't have gender parity in their salaries, women will continue to be seen as *"less than"*.

When women are not recruited into drug trials because their bodies are seen as *"too complicated"* and will *"skew the data"*, women will continue to lack access to effective drugs and treatments.

When women are dismissed and disbelieved by the medical profession, the medical care of women will be inadequate.

When boys, men, girls and women make false accusations of abuse and are not held to account, victim-survivors are less likely to be believed.

When men refuse to access counselling or other support services because they have been conditioned to believe that *"men are strong"* or they should *"man up"*, we will continue to have a crisis of male violence, mental ill health and suicide.

When childhood and generational trauma is not recognised, funded and integrated as a whole of society response, we will continue to create perpetrators and victim-survivors of violence.

When people with disabilities are not adequately cared for, supported, and given a voice and autonomy, they will continue to be vulnerable and prey for abusers.

When governments continue to not adequately recognise, fund and support victims of institutionalised abuse, whether it be the stolen generation or those who have been in any kind of residential "care", we will continue to "create" perpetrators and victims of violence.

When the government itself perpetuates gender stereotypes and does not have equal representation of men and women, women will continue to be diminished.

The list of issues that contribute to domestic violence is endless. The only way that domestic violence will be effectively curtailed is when the whole of society, in unison, shouts, ***"Enough is enough"***.

When our entire community commits to understanding the anatomy of domestic violence, to working collaboratively, to having uncomfortable conversations, to holding people to account and to tearing down the walls of shame, then maybe, just maybe, we might be able to end domestic violence.

SEVENTEEN

Emily's story was never going to be *"happy ever after"*, but I had hoped the burdens she carried would have abated once she moved into her own little flat and started to build, once again, a life for herself. Sadly, they haven't.

When Emily was beginning her cancer journey, as is usual, she had some blood tests. What she wasn't expecting, out of the blue, was a diagnosis of Hemochromatosis. It doesn't always have a genetic cause, but in Emily's case, it does. Both of her parents had the faulty gene and passed it down to Emily. Once she had the blood test results, her whole genetic family had to be tested. Unfortunately, her sons also have the condition, but so far, they are fine. The disorder involves a dangerous build-up of iron in the liver, which can then impact all the systems in the body, including liver damage, heart problems, diabetes and arthritis.

Due to Emily's chronic alcohol misuse, the symptoms of Hemochromatosis have been exacerbated. Her liver is suffering the ill effects of both the disease and alcohol. She has chronic arthritis and has developed osteoporosis. Emily seems to break a bone if she so much as sneezes when she's in the wrong position. I have lost count of the number of bones that Emily has broken: her collarbone, her arm, her hip, her femur. She has spinal damage, so she can't move her head or back particularly well and sitting for too long is painful. She needs a crutch to help her walk, and if she has far to go, she requires a wheelchair. Her teeth have crumbled as a result of the osteoporosis, and she has been waiting on consent from her children to access her funds for orthodontic treatment. So far, they have refused because they view it as "cosmetic". Something their father has clearly said to them. They have also told Emily they won't release any funds to her to improve her flat until her current partner has moved out. It is outrageous that a woman in her fifties has to ask permission from her children to spend her own money.

Missing her daughter's graduation was bad enough, but her children are all now in long-term relationships. Her daughter got married a few years ago, and she told her mum she didn't want her there. Emily was devastated once more. Recently, Hannah gave birth to twins. Emily has seen photos of them, which she has shared with me but Hannah hasn't allowed her to see them. Ellis and Patrick are soon to be married. Emily has no idea if they will invite her to their weddings. Her father's message continues to be that Emily is dangerous. He has told her that she shouldn't let Emily see the babies because she will harm them.

Emily is often sober for short periods of time, but she is desperately vulnerable. Whilst she is fully committed to being sober, I wonder whether she will ever fully manage it. I sincerely hope that she does. She is committed to getting back into the workforce in some way. She wants to be productive, and there is a level of self-esteem that being in the workforce brings. Finding a suitable job, though, is almost impossible. Writing this book has been therapeutic for Emily, and through the process, I have seen her mental health increase little by little, day by day. For now, she is sober. I'm so relieved she's in a much better place.

Every time she hears her children repeating words she has heard so many times from her abuser, it hits her like a wrecking ball, and she starts to drink again. I have no doubt Emily's children love her deeply and are also worried about their mother, but a lifetime of lies and manipulation from their father has given them a completely false image of their mum. They are also fatigued by the multiple crises Emily has gone through.

Emily and I had made a decision to write this book, but it took us a few months to organise ourselves. In mid-2024, I began to interview her. In fact, I was on my way to see her when I received a phone call from her number. I answered, expecting her to ask me what time I was arriving and what kind of cake I wanted. I was in an area with dodgy mobile phone coverage, so the phone dropped out.

All I understood was, *"Hello, my name's Joe. I'm a paramedic."* I cannot find the words to describe the cold fear that flowed through me. I tried to call back. No connection. Then my phone rang again but disconnected. My heart was in my mouth. Then I got a text message that came through to my car's entertainment system. *"Hi, I'm Joe, I'm a paramedic. I'm just taking Emily to the hospital. She stepped in a pothole on the way to get milk for your morning tea, and we're a bit concerned she might have broken her ankle. She told me you were on your way, so she asked me to call you to let you know."* My relief was palpable.

I detoured to the local hospital. By the time I got there, Emily had been put in a little room in the Emergency Department. She was waiting for x-rays. Just as Emily laughed at me when she called me leaving Emergency at the very start of this process, I laughed at her tripping up on a pothole. Like old friends do, we teased each other about our ageing bodies. Knowing how long it takes in an Emergency Department, we took advantage of the private room and set about our first interview for this book, which I recorded.

Fortunately, Emily hadn't fractured her ankle; it was just a bad sprain. I took her home, I made the tea, and we talked for a few more hours. Whilst I knew about most of the events, it was an opportunity for Emily to give me the details. As is usual with someone who is traumatised, Emily found it difficult to recall exact dates. Together, we used our joint recollections to put together a timeline. I have recorded multiple interviews with Emily since that time, in person and via video calls. We can only talk for short periods of time because the content of our calls is so painful. Whilst Emily has endured the abuse for decades, talking about the incidents and her abuser's pattern of behaviour whilst I clarify the details compresses the stories into an intense narrative.

Hearing Emily tell her story has been distressing. On the one hand, I listened to her recounting the decades of horrific abuse, and I just wanted to hold my friend in my arms and comfort her. On the other hand, I had a job to do, and I had to document her story so that together, the community could be educated about the anatomy of domestic violence. I had to hold my personal distress and my professional detachment in each hand. At one point, I asked a close psychologist friend and colleague if she could provide me with clinical supervision so that I could share the burden with another human. So that I could, metaphorically, be held and cared for. Domestic violence is traumatic for everyone.

Emily has found a supportive therapist who I hope will be able to assist her in processing her life events and the constant and long-term abuse she has endured. Emily is never far from my thoughts. Worrying about her has become my default position. I find part of my heart constantly dreads a devastating phone call. Nevertheless, I remind myself that Emily is the most resilient and courageous woman I know. She has defiantly refused to let her life be defined by her abuser.

Despite her broken body and extensive trauma, the young woman I met all of those years ago is still there. When we catch up, either in person or via video, the light in her eyes is still there. She is still funny and caring. The last time I saw her, we went out for lunch. We passed a random statue of some men. There was no plaque, so we had no idea what the statue represented. Emily decided to swing around a nearby pole, deposit herself on the lap of one of the bronze men and pretend to have a conversation with him. She still has the capacity to drop her chin and whisper conspiratorially about some piece of gossip or say something wildly inappropriate. She is still enchanted by literature, theatre and history. She loves her children unconditionally and is so proud of them that she could almost burst. She is furious about the state of the world, the environment and politics. She worries about women who have experienced domestic violence and other vulnerable members of the community.

I love Emily unconditionally, and I know that she loves me unconditionally, too. She is, quite simply, my best friend.

RESOURCES

- **1800RESPECT**
  National domestic, family and sexual violence counselling, information and support service.
  Phone: 1800 737 732 or sms 0458 737 732.
  www.1800respect.org.au

- **13YARN**
  Aboriginal and Torres Strait Islander counselling services are run by Aboriginal and Torres Strait Islander people.
  Phone 13 92 76.
  www.13yarn.org.au

- **ANROWS**
  Australia's National Research Organisation for Women's Safety. Research organisation that supports ending violence against women and children in Australia.
  www.anrows.org.au

- **Beyond Blue Support Service**
  Free and confidential telephone counselling 24/7.
  Phone 1300 22 4636.
  www.beyondblue.org.au

- **Family Relationship Advice Line**
  National telephone service that helps families affected by relationship or separation issues. Phone 1800 050 321.
  www.familyrelationships.gov.au

- **Keeping Kids In Mind**
  Parenting course facilitated across Australia by trained and experienced practitioners with small groups of separated parents.
  www.keepingkidsinmind.org

- **Lifeline Australia**
  Crisis support and suicide prevention counselling 24/7.
  Phone 13 11 14.
  www.lifeline.org.au

- **Mensline Australia**
  Free 24/7 counselling service for men.
  Phone 1300 789 978.
  www.mensline.org.au

- **Men's Referral Service**
  National counselling information and referral service for men looking to change their behaviour.
  Phone 1300 766 491.

- **No to Violence**
  Peak Body for organisations and individuals who work with men to end family violence.
  Phone 1300 766 491.
  www.ntv.org.au

- **Safe and Together Institute**
  Courses, training and tools to equip practitioners working with perpetrators and victim-survivors of domestic violence.
  www.safeandtogether.com

- **White Ribbon Australia**
  Part of the global White Ribbon movement engaging men and boys to reduce future incidences of violence, promote gender equality and start positive, respectful relationships.
  www.whiteribbonaustralia.org.au

ABOUT THE
AUTHOR

Angharad worked at the "pointy end" of community services as a psychologist, supervisor and leader in a large NGO for over three decades. She often says she is completely unshockable and has seen it all: child protection, domestic violence, trauma, grief, parenting and child development. She loved every minute of it.

She medically retired from permanent work at the end of 2023 due to the dual impact of Multiple Sclerosis and Psoriatic Arthritis, but she certainly wasn't going to put her feet up. Instead, she has continued to train practitioners, speak at conferences and events and has turned her hand to writing to continue serving the community.

The Anatomy of Domestic Violence: Emily's story is her second solo work. Her first book Bugger, Bugger, Shit: my quest for resilience (Morpheus Publishing 2024), told her own story. This book is a testament to friendship; it is the story of one of her closest friends.

Angharad is about to embark on her third book, The House of Lost Souls. This time, she will explore the issue of complex trauma as she tells the story of another of her closest friends. It is due for release in 2026.

To find more about Angharad, read her blogs or book her to speak at an event or facilitate training, you can check out her website www. angharadcandlin.com

ACKNOWLEDGEMENTS

Emily's Acknowledgements

I want to say thank you to the strong women in my life: my mother, my grandmother, my sister, all of my friends, and especially Jen. They have all supported me through this life, and without their love, care and acceptance, I don't think I'd still be alive.

Angharad's Acknowledgements

I wish this book hadn't been written. I wish Emily didn't have a story to tell. I wish every victim-survivor didn't have a story, and I wish every murdered woman were still alive. But... Emily does have a story and it had to be written, both for her and for every victim-survivor.

"Emily" is my brave, beautiful, amazing friend and kindred spirit. You are loved beyond measure. You trusted me. I hold that preciously in the palms of my hands and in the folds of my heart. I honour you.

"Ellis", "Hannah", "Patrick", and "Hugh", this book is for you, with my love forever. I am and will always be here for you.

Lynette, your editing skills really are your superpower. When I couldn't find the right words, when I struggled to find the best way to describe situations, you came to my rescue. I cannot thank you enough for your unwavering commitment behind the scenes to ensuring Emily's story was told in the absolutely best way possible. Thank you for your bravery in being the first to read every raw, unedited word and being able to rise above your emotions to bring clarity and excellence to this manuscript.

Justine, my publisher, has championed me since our very first conversation. Thank you for your continuing support and your commitment to elevating the voices of vulnerable people.

Margaret, thank you so much for being hands when I needed them, being outraged along with me and making me laugh just at the right moments.

Sam, I loved working with you to bring 'Safe and Together' front and centre in all of our practice. Your passion for the work we do and your commitment to our clients is inspiring. Thank you for holding me accountable for my language and for being so enthusiastic about grabbing my hand so we could leap into the water together.

My family, thank you for putting up with me and for taking my banishments when I'm writing with good grace. Thank you for your commitment to ending domestic violence and for your passion for social justice.

Sara, Jackie and Jonathan, our friendship and your support of my writing are never taken for granted. Thank you for allowing me to rant on and for the big conversations we always find ourselves having. You fill my cup.

Jonathan, thank you for your patience with my completely un-mathematical brain, for your ongoing willingness to be my male sounding board and for your unwavering principles regarding ethical behaviour and gender equity.

David Mandel, Ruth Raymundo Mandel and the Safe and Together Institute, words cannot express my gratitude for the work that you do. Your training transformed my practice and gave me the keys to write this book.

To all the warriors who continually hold up mirrors to society and call for an end to domestic violence, thank you for your passion and commitment.

To every single victim-survivor of domestic violence: you are valued, you are respected, you are brave, you have immeasurable strengths, and you deserve better. We all failed you, and I'm so very sorry.

www.ingramcontent.com/pod-product-compliance
Lightning Source LLC
Chambersburg PA
CBHW051246020426
42333CB00025B/3072